**Crossing the Bar
Head
Our Lady of Shadows**

Seren Drama

*Dannie Abse: The View from Row G
Laurence Allan: On the Road Again (three plays)
Phil Clark (ed): Act One Wales
Lucinda Coxon: Waiting at the Water's Edge
Greg Cullen: Mary Morgan (three plays)
Dic Edwards: The Shakespeare Factory (three plays)
Peter Lloyd: The Scam
Edward Thomas: House of America (three plays)
Gwyn Thomas: Three Plays
Charles Way: Dead Man's Hat*

LUCY GOUGH

**Crossing the Bar
Head
Our Lady of Shadows**

seren

seren
is the book imprint of
Poetry Wales Press Ltd
Wyndham Street, Bridgend, Wales

© Lucy Gough, 2000

The right of Lucy Gough to be identified as the Author
of this Work has been asserted in accordance with the
Copyright, Designs and Patents Act 1988.

ISBN 1-85411-266-X

A CIP record for this title is available from
the British Library

All rights reserved. No part of this publication
may be reproduced, stored in a retrieval system,
or transmitted at any time or by any means
electronic, mechanical, photocopying, recording
or otherwise without the prior permission
of the copyright holder.

*The publisher works with the financial assistance of the
Arts Council of Wales*

Cover Design: Andy Dark

Printed in Palatino by
WBC Book Manufacturers, Bridgend

Contents

- 7   Crossing The Bar
- 53   Head
- 83   Our Lady Of Shadows

- 113   *Acknowledgements*
- 114   *About the Author*

Crossing the Bar

Crossing the Bar was first performed by the Fallen Angel Theatre Company on with the following cast:

CHARACTERS

NUN	Jenny Livsey
BOY	Rhydian Jones
KEEPER/GAOLER	Rhodri John
Directed by	Ashley Wallington

BOY: A young lad from Swansea. He has 'Cut Here' tattooed on his neck.

NUN: A young novice Nun from the Middle-Ages. She is dressed in a simple white habit. The Nun's language is written phonetically.

Act One
SCENE ONE

(*Setting:* The action of the play takes place in that instant on the border between life and death. There is a cell [in Dread] with a single door and a high barred window. A bare, lit lightbulb hangs in the centre and there is also the broken end of a sheet rope hanging from the ceiling. There are two candles burning in a window-box on one wall. The bell that is heard has a tone as if it has been slowed down from its proper recorded speed, until the final scene.

An alarm bell sounds very loudly. In the corner the NUN is sitting very still watching something moving across the floor. The BOY is wandering around the cell obviously disorientated. He is wearing a pair of baggy white underpants and has a broken sheet rope around his neck. The BOY occasionally touches things and is vaguely looking for something. Suddenly the NUN slams her hand on the floor and catches a cockroach she has been watching. She then puts it in her mouth and starts crunching it.)

BOY: (*to NUN*) Not again?

(*The BOY continues to pace and search.*)

BOY: The same?

(*to NUN*)

Do you have to?

8

CROSSING THE BAR

(*touching the walls and bed, etc.*)

The fuckin' same, even the fucking wallpaper's the same.

(*BOY pacing. NUN catches a cockroach, as she goes to eat it BOY dives at her and hits it out of her hand.*)

I said....

NUN: Mybody be sterved!

BOY: (*to her face*) The fuckin' same, all the fuckin' same.

(*NUN reaches for cockroach. He stamps on it.*)

NUN: Mybody be sterved.

BOY: 'Cept for you, 'cept for Hannibal the Cannibal. (*He walks around again in despair.*) All of it, after all that. All that.

(*The NUN smoothes her hands over her breasts and then over her body. The BOY finds his shirt and pulls it on.*)

NUN: It be the fastygne.

BOY: All that, and it's the fucking same.

NUN: The fastygne rente my flesh.

(*BOY goes to cell window and looks out. NUN gets up in search of cockroaches.*)

BOY: Even this! Even this the fucking same! Black. Same fucking black, same stars, boring fucking stars, hundreds of the fuckers. All the same!

NUN: (*as she hunts for cockroaches*) In my nyght I wynde mybody to the stars.

BOY: Going on forever, forever, like this, forever and ever.

NUN: I peer into Hevene.

(*BOY goes to door and starts banging on it.*)

CROSSING THE BAR

BOY: You can't do this! Not this, not forever. Not forever and ever. I got rights even 'ere. I got rights, get the guvner, get 'im.

(*He challenges the NUN who is talking to herself and completely unconcerned by BOY.*)

Who runs this shithole?

NUN: (*more to herself*) But it be not the image of this.

BOY: I said who?

NUN: Wolde image.

BOY: Like talking to a monkey! (*banging loudly on the door*) Come on! There must be some fucker out there, someone must run this fucking place, someone, someone better come 'ere soon. I gotta sort this out, it's driving me fucking crazy man, it ain't fair, not fucking fair, not this, not this. All that I did, all that, not to land here, not to land up in the same fucking place.

(*NUN leaps on another cockroach, catches it and holds it up, triumphant.*)

NUN: Body and blood! (*puts it in her mouth*)

BOY: (*grabs NUN*) Sick, you're fucking sick!

NUN: (*defiant*) Wynde me to Hell? Come ye to quelle me? Stampe mybody. Rente me to pieces? Pull mybody into the fyr.

BOY: What shit is this?

NUN: Shit?

BOY: Shit, you talk shit.

NUN: Speke shit?

BOY: Yeah.

NUN: Be thee from Hevene or Hell?

BOY: (*lets go of her*) How the fuck should I know?

CROSSING THE BAR

(*NUN starts her hunting again. BOY blocks her way.*)

BOY: You could kill 'em first, you could at least do that.

SCENE TWO

(*The BOY is inspecting the broken end of rope. The NUN is looking around.*)

NUN: Mybody lieth in a place the image of this! But I felt myself slide from my body like shit from a hole.

BOY: Do you reckon it broke? That it broke?

NUN: Myself beheld mybody.

BOY: That feeling.

NUN: Myself beheld it, the lyfe sterved from mybody.

BOY: And nothing changed, nothing, 'cept you and the quiet, the fucking quiet. I hate quiet, it means, it means....

NUN: How can mybody have faith in my belief without beholding Hym?

BOY: It's all the same, but dead, dead quiet, what the fuck is this?!

NUN: Mybody blaked to beholde Hym!

BOY: If it's the same, but different, the same as before but different, then....

NUN: Mybody trespassed to beholde Hym.

BOY: If it's different out there, no fuckers out there, then we don't have to stay 'ere, in 'ere! (*directly to NUN*) We can get out, get the fuck out, nothing keeping us 'ere. Maybe there's a whole fucking world out there, waiting, the fucking lot.

NUN: Thyn gate concealeth Hevene or Hell.

11

CROSSING THE BAR

BOY: Out there?
NUN: Yea.
BOY: You reckon?
NUN: Mybody believes this be purgatory.
BOY: You what?
NUN: Purgatory.
BOY: What the fuck's that?
NUN: Thyn body know not!
BOY: 'Course I do, (*bluffs*) it's where you go.... (*silence*) So what happen's now? What do they do next?
NUN: Our souls be cleansed.
BOY: How long does that take?

(*silence*)

NUN: As long as it be.
BOY: Bit like a launderette then, you just wait till it's finished.
NUN: If yon can bear it.

(*silence*)

BOY: What's outside that door?
NUN: Hevene and Hell.
BOY: S'pose it's Heaven for you?
NUN: Mybody synned.
BOY: So we go together.

(*They start to move towards the door. The NUN stops.*)

NUN: Why not stay within?
BOY: Might be better than here. (*He moves towards the door again.*) We could just have a look.

12

CROSSING THE BAR

NUN: Hell be grisly, a great hole with flames, thye can witness the screams of the wretched souls.

BOY: (*He stops.*) Maybe later. (*He listens by the door.*) Nothing. I can't hear nothing.

NUN: Thyn gate doeth conceal it.

BOY: What makes you the expert? How come you know so much?

NUN: Hevene and Hell arrived on wagons.

BOY: You what?

NUN: To my village, Hevene be trussed with angels to the roof.

BOY: This supposed to make sense?

NUN: But mybody behooldeth not Hym visage.

BOY: You been 'ere a long time or something?

NUN: (*trying hard to make the BOY understand*) Hym visage, (*she gestures to her face*) Hym visage, mybody nat woot Hym hewe. (*She is getting upset because he doesn't understand.*) Mybody nay sayn mine Fadder in Hevene, nay sayn Hym visage.

BOY: Done for you, has it? Being here.

NUN: But Hell be terrible, feends spit bile and....

BOY: ...That's it. That's it! I've had enough, ain't it time you had dinner? (*He points to floor. BOY moves back to door and listens.*) Nothing, nothing, not a thing, not a fucking thing. I'd hear it if there was a fucking great fire behind that.

(*NUN has moved over to bed and is looking at it.*)

NUN: Mybody did lieth upon a bed the image of this one, flesh turning to bone. (*She gets onto the bed and lies down.*) Gobets of bread were offered as the Sisters devysed to cure mybody, and sweatmeats. But none woldest them here of my desire, so lay

CROSSING THE BAR

	mybody down and slipped out, flesh turning bone, slipped out slowly like a great turd from mybody.
	(*BOY walks towards her. He is excited now.*)
BOY:	Like one of those mega-shits, you know, when it's all stacked up and it hurts to get it out? Well, fuck me, if you'd told me that, told me before, dying was like having a crap. (*He stops.*) But it fucking hurt, it fucking hurt, it hurt like Hell.

SCENE THREE

	(*BOY is exercising. NUN is still lying on the bed.*)
NUN:	(*She sits up.*) Whatso ydoon?
BOY:	Nothing.
NUN:	Why hurl thyn limb, be thy apoplexie?
BOY:	Nothing, I'm doing nothing. (*still exercising*) I'm doing nothing.
	(*NUN lies down again.*)
NUN:	Mybody also.
	(*Silence. BOY still exercising. NUN starts to say her rosary.*)
NUN:	Holy Magdelene intercede for my soul. Holy Felicitas intercede for my soul. Holy Agatha intercede for my soul. Holy Martin intercede for my soul.
	(*BOY tries to ignore her by exercising even harder. Finally, he can't take it and snaps at her.*)
BOY:	What the fuck you doing?
NUN:	Nothyng.
BOY:	That noise.

14

CROSSING THE BAR

NUN: Nothyng. Mybody ydoon nothyng. (*carries on with rosary*) Mybody ydoon nothyng.

BOY: It's a fucking racket, can't you do it quiet?

(*NUN continues rosary in a quieter tone which is even more irritating — a sort of rhythmic murmur. BOY [exercising] tries to ignore it. Finally, he goes for her.*)

BOY: Cut that out!

(*silence*)

That noise, your noise, makes me notice. Notice the quiet. Maybe Hell would be better than this. Maybe there's noise in Hell, lots of it.

NUN: Skriking.

BOY: Something to do.

NUN: Thybody racked.

BOY: Maybe I'll be on my fucking own.

NUN: Everemo.

BOY: Christ, it's got to be better than this.

NUN: Thider been nought but the image of before.

BOY: Different. Hell will be different. I'm going, I'm going to Hell. You coming?

NUN: Them feends prick arses with forks.

BOY: I don't fucking care.

NUN: Evermo, for everemo.

BOY: We got forever here, at least it won't be the same. (*He starts to walk towards the door.*) You coming?

NUN: Namo!

BOY: You gonna stay here?

NUN: Hell be grisly.

BOY: So's this.

CROSSING THE BAR

NUN: Thereby nought but peyne.

BOY: Here. In here there's pain, the pain of nothing, like a dead leg. Come on, (*puts his hand out*) together we can go together.

(*She moves towards him cautiously, takes his hand. They walk towards the door. He is still coaxing her. When they reach the door he suddenly takes control and as they reach it he pushes her in front.*)

BOY: Ladies first.

(*The door suddenly opens revealing a man in dark silhouette, a grotesque image. He shouts.*)

KEEPER: Never change!

(*They are startled. The KEEPER enters. He is holding a pair of trousers and speaks to the BOY very loudly.*)

KEEPER: Never change! (*He walks in and speaks in a more normal voice.*) Never change! I saw you. Ladies first! (*to NUN*) Never trust a man. Don't they teach you anything in these convents?

(*BOY and NUN have backed away.*)

BOY: Who the fuck are you?

KEEPER: Fuck?

BOY: Fuck!

KEEPER: Fuck. Not a word I come across often. (*to NUN*) Medieval, would you say?

BOY: You what?

KEEPER: (*to NUN*) Know that word, do you? (*NUN hides behind BOY.*) I wouldn't bother. Not him. (*hands BOY the trousers*) Steam cleaned.

(*BOY takes trousers.*)

BOY: What?

KEEPER: Mucky pup. I hate people who die messy.

CROSSING THE BAR

BOY: What you saying?

KEEPER: Caked on it was.

(*BOY is embarrassed.*)

BOY: I never did. I never.

KEEPER: Hanging does funny things to the body.

BOY: I never did!

(*BOY puts his trousers on. He feels better so he again challenges the KEEPER.*)

BOY: Who the fuck are you?

KEEPER: Nobody you know.

BOY: Don't be clever.

KEEPER: Why not?

BOY: Just don't.

KEEPER: (*to NUN*) Getting enough to eat?

BOY: How come she eats?

KEEPER: You get steam cleaned.

BOY: Will those fucking roaches ever stop?

KEEPER: They like this sort of place.

BOY: What sort of place is this?

KEEPER: Some know it as *Dread*.

NUN: Wende thee from Hevene or from Hell?

KEEPER: None or the other.

BOY: What the fuck does that mean?

NUN: Have thou sayn Hym visage?

KEEPER: I see 'em all, who do you mean particularly?

BOY: *Dread*, what the fuck does that mean? *Dread*.

NUN: God.

CROSSING THE BAR

KEEPER: We've shared a jar on one or two occasions.

BOY: What sort of name is that? *Dread*?

NUN: Whatso of Hym image?

KEEPER: Like God.

BOY: I'm talking to you.

NUN: Be it the image of my Fadder.

KEEPER: Well, he is your Fadder so to speak.

NUN: I mean my Fadder.

BOY: I've got a pair of fucking monkeys in here now. *Dread*? What do it mean?

KEEPER: Solpe Ipus.

BOY: Supposed to understand that, am I?

KEEPER: Himself alone.

NUN: Woldest thou carry mybody to Hym?

KEEPER: Can't do that.

NUN: In my nyght I wende mybody to the stars and peer in to Hevene.

KEEPER: What you do in your dreams is your business.

BOY: He can't take you cause it don't exist.

KEEPER: Someone rattling your cage?

BOY: True though, can't show her something that don't exist.

KEEPER: You believe in Hell?

BOY: Possibly.

KEEPER: If there's Hell there must be Heaven.

BOY: If you've seen him, seen him here. Then he must be dead too like us, so if he was there before he ain't now, he's dead. God is dead. Nothing, like us nothing.

CROSSING THE BAR

KEEPER: One cries "I seek God", the other, "He's dead".
NUN: Mybody begges. Kanstow carry me to Hevene?
KEEPER: I can't do that.
NUN: Whyso?
KEEPER: In the book it says you sinned. Trespassed.
NUN: Nat but to mineself, nat but to mineself.
KEEPER: You took a life.
NUN: Mine own.
KEEPER: Still murder.
NUN: To behoold Hym, I sterved mybody to sayn Hym.
KEEPER: You committed yourself.
BOY: Yes, but to what?
NUN: To sayn Hym.
BOY: What we committed to?
KEEPER: Expectation. The expectation of society.
BOY: Fuck off!
NUN: I committed mybody to God.
BOY: She carries him round like a dead dog, "Mybody wants, mybody needs."

(*The NUN suddenly knees him in the balls. He falls to the floor groaning. The KEEPER and NUN watch him with interest. Eventually he can speak.*)

BOY: Bitch! (*still lying on the floor*) Dying was the only thing I ever done.
KEEPER: It was the only thing you hadn't done.
NUN: (*points at BOY*) From wende this shit?
KEEPER: A century that deals in shit more than your own.
NUN: Come he to punish me?

CROSSING THE BAR

BOY: I did my own death, I did it!

KEEPER: It was a collective crime, lack of care. Society was your midwife and executioner.

BOY: I found a way out.

KEEPER: Well, now you know you haven't.

(*KEEPER goes to the candles and tends them like flowers. BOY gets up.*)

BOY: Expecting a power cut?

KEEPER: Lighten your darkness.

BOY: But it ain't dark.

KEEPER: Inside.

BOY: Inside what?

KEEPER: You.

BOY: Yeah, it's dark in there alright, pitch dark, so what will these do? Eh!

KEEPER: Not for me to say.

NUN: Mybody deyde to behoolde, but it be concealed everemo.

BOY: (*to KEEPER*) Where do we go next?

KEEPER: Next? Next to what?

BOY: To this. Where do we go after?

KEEPER: After. After what?

BOY: Stop pissing me around, what happens next? Do I have to pay?

KEEPER: Pay?

BOY: Pay for what I done?

KEEPER: Next. After. Done. Next, after, done, words heavy with time.

20

CROSSING THE BAR

BOY: But I want to know what's coming.

KEEPER: Look where wanting to know got her.

NUN: I had to have feith in my beliefe, I had to.

(BOY spots that the door is open. He edges over and tries to look out.)

BOY: I can't see nothing awful, no flames, no devils. No screams!

KEEPER: Whatever your mind can conceive. *(The bell is heard. The KEEPER starts to leave.)* Someone's soul seeking its existence.

(The BOY paces in despair, kicks a wall and then slides down in despair.)

BOY: Fucking Hell.

(The BOY puts his head in his hands and the NUN walks over to the window.)

SCENE FOUR

(BOY is sitting on the floor, head in hands. NUN is looking out of the window.)

BOY: Fucking bored. I'm fucking bored, fucking bored.

NUN: There's a man on the erythe espies the stars with a glass.

BOY: Fucking bored, bored, bored.

(BOY gets up and starts pacing around sniffing. The NUN has farted and the BOY cannot work out what the smell is.)

NUN: Espies the stars with a glass.

BOY: *(as he sniffs under the bed)* I can see the stars. I can see them, you can see them, and they're fucking boring. Fucking boring, like you, like this place.

CROSSING THE BAR

NUN: Holde fast to them, abide betwixt and between them.

BOY: What the fuck you want to be up there for? Do you reckon they're trying to gas us. That smell?

NUN: And gold.

BOY: Fuck off! There ain't nothing up there, nothing 'cept rocks and holes. It's fucking boring. I seen it on the telly and its fucking boring. Can you smell it, that smell?

NUN: Aye, thyn behoolden Hevene?

BOY: Just rocks. Rocks and holes. I told you, Heaven ain't there, it's like Father Christmas. Made up! Where the fuck does it come from that smell? (*agitated*) What if? Where the fuck's it coming from?

NUN: My arse. (*She lifts up her habit and takes a deep breath.*) Fart but no turd.

BOY: Fucking disgusting.

NUN: Where be my Fadder?

BOY: Rotting like the rest of us.

NUN: No! He be in Hevene. Mybody dremed this.

BOY: I dream my body is a clock. Tick, tick, fucking tick.

NUN: Mybody clymbeth a ladder to the stars.

BOY: My arms stretched round my face.

NUN: And there espie Hym visage.

BOY: My heart beating out the seconds.

NUN: But mybody nat know Hym be my Fadder on erthye or my Fadder in Hevene.

BOY: Tick, tick, fucking tick. (*gets angry*) For fuck's sake, shut up about your Father. I got one of those and he's a waste of space.

CROSSING THE BAR

NUN: Be he in Hevene?

BOY: No! Go to Hell. (*He points to the door.*)

NUN: What rages thyn?

BOY: Shut it.

NUN: Be thy afeared?

BOY: No!

NUN: Never a deel?

BOY: What's to be scared of? There's nothing 'ere.

NUN: Fear holdes fast to me.

BOY: Do you reckon they can see us? (*looks in corners of the cell for cameras*) Reckon they're watching us now? Like they do in the Arcades? (*shouts at imaginary cameras*) Watching us, eh? Watching us? To see if we shit ourselves. How long we been here? Do you reckon there's Clocks in Hell?

NUN: Just fyr skriking, soore pyne and the devile farting.

BOY: You reckon it's full of little devils with horns and forks. Bloody daft, it won't be like that. It'll be full of coppers and screws and electrodes. And when you're hot they turn the heating up and when you're cold they'll turn it down.

(*The bell sounds.*)

BOY: Someone trying to find out the time.

SCENE FIVE

(*BOY is in a corner doing something suspicious looking. The NUN is looking up bemused but intently at the corner of the ceiling.*)

BOY: Anything?

CROSSING THE BAR

NUN: Nothyng.

BOY: You sure?

NUN: Aye.

BOY: Nothing?

NUN: Nothyng.

(*KEEPER enters.*)

KEEPER: Passing time?

BOY: I told you. Didn't I? I told you! (*to KEEPER*) Come to see what I'm doing, weren't you?

KEEPER: What you do here is your concern, affects no-one but you.

BOY: You were watching us, you must have been.

KEEPER: No need.

BOY: Don't you want to know what I was doing?

KEEPER: No.

BOY: Guess?

KEEPER: It matters not.

BOY: I was digging my way out. There's a tunnel through there. I was nearly out. Nearly out!

KEEPER: Your soul clings like a monkey.

BOY: You what?

KEEPER: Clings terrified like a man held over a precipice.

BOY: (*anxiously*) I can't see it? (*starts to shake himself and brush himself off as if something is clinging to him*) You taking the piss?

NUN: Has the torture begun?

BOY: She's sick, you know, sick. Eats roaches and farts.

KEEPER: She has to pass out the sins that she's eaten.

CROSSING THE BAR

BOY: But the smell.
KEEPER: Evil was pungent then.
NUN: What sin is there?
KEEPER: That question is weighted.
BOY: I don't understand.
KEEPER: Words?
BOY: They don't make sense.
KEEPER: That's the beauty of words. Violence isn't necessary when one has words. Did your life make sense?
BOY: I thought...
KEEPER: ...Death would bring meaning.
BOY: I weren't going to say that.
KEEPER: I pre-empt.
BOY: You're doing it again! Talking shit.
KEEPER: There's a solitude in words with no meaning, a liturgy in limbo.
BOY: Stop it, stop it! Ain't it enough that you got me banged up here?
KEEPER: Circumscribed by lack of vision.
BOY: You're doing it again! What the fuck does that mean?
KEEPER: Use the door. Why not use the door?
BOY: I ain't going out there.
KEEPER: Why not?
BOY: She told me.
KEEPER: The medieval mind is very fertile.
BOY: You mean it ain't out there?

CROSSING THE BAR

KEEPER: Might not be.

BOY: It ain't out there?

KEEPER: Find out.

BOY: You promise. You mean she made it up. (*turns to NUN*) You made it up?

NUN: No!

BOY: It don't exist either.

KEEPER: Find out.

(*BOY goes to the door.*)

BOY: This a trick?

KEEPER: Do I look like a magician?

(*The BOY opens the door and cautiously looks out then takes a step over the threshold. He immediately screams and runs back in and over to the bed and puts the blanket over his head. The KEEPER laughs.*)

KEEPER: Hell got worse over the centuries, has it? (*to NUN*) Ask him, ask him what it looks like?

(*The KEEPER leaves.*)

NUN: Pray speke, seyn folk peyned? Seyn thy fyr? Thy body shente by feends? Speke? Did thyn feend skriken at thyn, rente they fleshe?

(*BOY stays under the blanket.*)

BOY: It ain't that, it ain't that, you don't understand, it's worse, much worse. I ain't going out there, not ever. Not ever. (*NUN gets onto the bed with him.*) They can't make us, can they? They can't make us.

SCENE SIX

(*NUN and BOY are attempting to race cockroaches. The BOY is trying to keep his in a straight line, with difficulty.*)

CROSSING THE BAR

BOY: This is fucking stupid! (*silence*) Fucking stupid! There. (*He points at the finish line.*) There, you stupid black bastard, there! Fuck me, how big does it have to be? Every fucking where but there! (*as he tries to steer it back on path*) A loser, I get the loser, come on!

NUN: (*as she watches hers going in the right direction*) A soul in flight, driven by desire, its little legs....

BOY: (*The BOY'S cockroach heads for the bed which is the wrong direction.*) Not there, you stupid fucker, not there! (*It goes under the bed, the BOY follows.*) No sense of direction, no ambition! (*BOY reappears, despondent.*)

NUN: My beetle won!

BOY: (*BOY stamps on it.*) Not now.

NUN: (*angry*) God don't whinge and whine all time, sayn black in allthings, God don't skrike on the vision of Hell, trembling as a fallen aungel, thy be more vile than Hell, more vile.

(*BOY lets out a huge roar and charges at the NUN. He pins her against the wall and then starts spinning her around. They spin faster and faster with the BOY occasionally roaring until they finally fall onto the floor.*)

NUN (*After a long silence.*) In fall forever, forever in fall.

BOY: It's what you fear. What you fear most is what you get. That's it. That's all there is. You'll never see him, never.

NUN: No!

BOY: Being dead is very long, if I could shit, it'd break it up a bit.

NUN: My bowels be full of beetles, but none breach my arse.

CROSSING THE BAR

BOY: If I could pile this place up with shit, I could count them.

NUN: Mybody feels them wriggle, but therebe nought for them in my belly, it be empty long before I died.

BOY: Mounds of shit, a shit a day or is it two, the length of a turd.

NUN: My wolde be spinning.

BOY: One way to make the earth move.

(*BOY gets up. As he does he looks at NUN lying on the floor as if he has seen her for the first time. He has realised she is a woman.*)

BOY: Reckon I should know you, reckon I should know your face.

(*As he looks the KEEPER suddenly appears again. He is carrying a measuring wheel of the type that are on a stick and which click every time it reaches the yard.*)

KEEPER: Transparent!

(*BOY moves out of his way.*)

KEEPER: Transparent.

BOY: Now what?

KEEPER: Your mind.

BOY: What about it?

KEEPER: What's in it.

(*The KEEPER starts to measure the cell with the wheel, counting to himself.*)

BOY: (*steps in front of him*) What you doing?

(*The KEEPER has lost count so he returns to the wall.*)

KEEPER: Health and safety. (*He starts to measure again, counting to himself. He reaches the BOY who stays in*

CROSSING THE BAR

his way.) Ten, remember ten.

(He walks round the boy and continues to measure. The BOY turns and follows behind him.)

BOY: I said, what you doing?

KEEPER: Eleven, what did I say to you?

BOY: Health.

KEEPER: What number did I give you?

BOY: I don't know, I don't care, what you up to? I thought they measured the body not the room.

(The KEEPER starts to measure the other way with BOY still following. The NUN is still lying on the floor. He wheels over her.)

KEEPER: Nasty beggars might take advantage, down there, don't those convents teach you anything?

NUN: Mybody be spinning.

BOY: I said. *(KEEPER reaches end and starts to work something out, ignoring the BOY.)* Tell me, vanished have I?

KEEPER: Transparent. *(attends to the candles, again like flowers)* Can squeeze another one in there. *(to BOY)* Should be fine, fine.

BOY: What? What you up to?

KEEPER: Room for one more.

BOY: In here?

KEEPER: Where else?

BOY: One more in here, you must be joking, there's only one bed!

KEEPER: Do you sleep?

BOY: Overcrowding, that's overcrowding.

KEEPER: I've worked it out, within the regulations. *Dread's*

29

CROSSING THE BAR

a very popular place, specially just now.

BOY: You can't do it, you can't. One more will drive me crazy.

KEEPER: Your state of mind is your concern. Not my job to recognise remorse.

(*The KEEPER goes back to candles and tenderly makes a gap between the two already there. The Bell rings.*)

BOY: It's going to be like a mass grave in 'ere, not healthy. (*NUN has sat up. BOY goes to her for support.*) He's bringing another in here with us, another.

NUN: What other?

BOY: One of us, another one of us, another body in 'ere, we'll be packed in like sardines.

NUN: What body? (*to KEEPER who is leaving*) Who?

BOY: She asked you a question, who?

KEEPER: That's for me to know and you to imagine.

BOY: Imagine?

KEEPER: The fear you desire or the desire you fear.

BOY: I fear nothing.

KEEPER: Your words own their deceit. Nothing changes, you learn to lose hope, to function between action and chainstoking, scared of living, scared of dying. In *Dread*. Hung. Charged with keeping a fragile balance.

(*The KEEPER leaves.*)

SCENE SEVEN

(*BOY is trying to move the bed. The NUN stands by indecisive as to whether to help him or not.*)

BOY: We can change things.

CROSSING THE BAR

NUN: Mybody thynketh nought.

BOY: Why not?

NUN: Hebe wroothful.

BOY: So what? (*pulling hard on the bed*) Come on, help.

NUN: He speke with God.

BOY: So fucking what, fuck the lot of them.

NUN: Not my God.

BOY: He ain't coming here. You gonna help or just stand there?

(*The NUN climbs onto the bed to prevent him from moving it.*)

NUN: Thou must move it nought, thou must nought move this! Hebe wroothful, mybody never beholde my Fadder.

BOY: What does it take? What? You're not just dead you're stupid, nothing's worth that much. You can't see it, can you? If we don't change things it will stay like this forever, forever. My life was like that, I don't want this to be. You heard him.

NUN: My hope is to beholde hym.

BOY: What the fuck is the point of seeing him? Come on, tell me, what's the point?

(*long pause*)

NUN: (*shouts*) How the fuck should I know? (*pause*) But mybody desire it longtime.

BOY: We have to change something. (*very persuasively*) Take the other end.

NUN: (*She gets off and starts to pull the bed.*) Thisbe not lightli.

BOY: Keep going. (*They struggle with the bed until they get it to the door where they place it across the doorway.*)

	There. Lock in, this 'ere is a lock in. (*He jumps onto the bed.*) Come on, sit here, body weight, he's built like a shit house. (*The BOY is excited and triumphant.*) Stuffed 'em we have, the lot. This will show 'em, this will.
NUN:	Shewe whom?
BOY:	SSSHHH! I can hear something, he's coming, he's coming. (*They wait, but nothing happens.*) He'll be here, he'll be here and I'll tell him "piss off, no room, no room in here".
NUN:	Thus spake the Taverner.
BOY:	Yeah, they say that a lot.
NUN:	And hebe Crist Jhesu.
BOY:	We definitely don't want none of his sort here. (*NUN has been looking over the edge of the bed and has now spotted something. She moves as if to get off the bed.*) Hang on, where you going? (*realizes what she is after*) Oh no! Not that, not that again, not here, not next to me. You gotta stay here.
NUN:	Forever?
BOY:	What else is there to do? Listen?
NUN:	Nothyng.
BOY:	He'll get here, he'll come and when he does! (*silence*) We have changed things, we have, the bed was there and now it's here.
NUN:	But noon other than this.
BOY:	But it was there.
NUN:	Ther biforn.
	(*She sees another cockroach and starts to lean over the side of the bed to try and catch it.*)
BOY:	No!

CROSSING THE BAR

NUN: Mybody begges!

BOY: No!

NUN: One.

BOY: He might come while you're off.

NUN: Mybody be sterved.

BOY: Go on then. If you start farting.... (*She dives off after a cockroach.*) I can hear him! (*She jumps back on with a cockroach and offers it to the BOY.*) Piss off! (*They wait listening, the BOY excitedly.*) We got him this time, we got him!

(*They wait and wait.*)

NUN: (*shouts suddenly*) Brynge out yon dead! Brynge out yon dead.

BOY: Shut it!

NUN: Brynge out yon dead!

BOY: What are you on about?

NUN: Brynge out yon dead! (*She sits herself on the front of the bed as if driving a cart.*) Brynge out yon dead!

BOY: What the fuck you playing at?

NUN: The man that gathered corpses on a wagon had hym visage forwrapped by blak cloth, so as I not beholde hym. Mybody thynketh, this be God. But somebody say God be my Fadder, so then mybody knew, my Fadder conceal hymself from me.

(*silence*)

BOY: Well, that got the place jumping. (*starts shouting*) Come on, you fuckers, come and see what we've done! Come on! Come on!

(*NUN sees another cockroach and leans over, the BOY stops her.*)

NUN: Mybody ydoon nothyg.

BOY: You ain't moving, he ain't getting the best of us, he ain't going to win. Don't you see, he ain't come 'cause he knows. Knows what we done and don't want us to know we've won. He'll have to come eventually.

NUN: Whyso?

BOY: He just will.

NUN: What then?

BOY: And then we'll see. We'll have him, we'll show him, change things. Change things.

(*BOY listens at the door. The NUN is watching for cockroaches.*)

SCENE EIGHT

(*Both are still on the bed but are now slumped with resignation as quite a long time has passed. Suddenly the KEEPER appears through a new doorway that opens in another part of the wall and startles them. He has a letter in one hand.*)

BOY: Where the fuck did you come from?

KEEPER: Here.

BOY: We blocked the door! We blocked it!

KEEPER: No!

BOY: We have! We fucking have!

KEEPER: Not here you haven't.

NUN: He be God.

KEEPER: I make no such claim.

(*He holds up the letter. The NUN goes to take it.*)

CROSSING THE BAR

BOY: Don't take it.
NUN: Whyso?
BOY: Just don't!
NUN: Whyso?
BOY: I said don't.
NUN: (*to KEEPER*) It be for me?
KEEPER: Could be.
NUN: For me from God.
BOY: Worse than a knife.

    (*The NUN takes the letter.*)

BOY: Marks the gut and the brain.
KEEPER: Here's someone who takes reality by the balls.
BOY: That what you call this? Reality?
KEEPER: On the cusp, astride possibility.
NUN: (*pointing at the letter*) What meaning this bear?
KEEPER: It's the way things are. Not otherwise but this.
BOY: So you say, who said we had to believe you?
KEEPER: Very simple, isn't it? Your problem.
BOY: I solved it.
KEEPER: Have you?
BOY: Yeah!
KEEPER: How?
BOY: I died.
KEEPER: You speak with such confidence.
BOY: Fuck off! Fuck off, it ain't got nothing to do with you.

    (*The NUN returns to the bed with the letter.*)

CROSSING THE BAR

NUN: Maybe it be from God, maybe it says....

BOY: ...Don't read it, don't.

NUN: Mybody blakes to know.

(*The BOY attempts to snatch the letter from her. He fails.*)

KEEPER: (*watching them he suddenly laughs*) The Owl and the Pussycat.

(*He leaves.*)

NUN: Whyso thy be wise, whyso thyn be wise in all thyngs and mybody be daft? I sterved mybody to see this man, maybe....

BOY: ...Have you ever seen anything with words, big words strung together like a fancy pattern with no beginning and no end, like a magic spell. People use words to frighten, they use them to hurt!

NUN: Somebe of bright hewe, maybe is sayn just one: "daughter".

BOY: Obsessed you are.

NUN: Maybe words be keys.

BOY: To lock you in.

(*She steels herself to open the letter. The BOY is sitting next to her trying not to look though he is tense and hunched. She opens it and reads, then cries out and throws it away in despair. Silence.*)

BOY: Well?

NUN: Nothyng.

BOY: Blank?

NUN: Nothyng.

BOY: No words?

CROSSING THE BAR

NUN: Nothyng.

(The BOY goes to the letter and braces himself, then picks it up and opens it. He reads it and suddenly starts laughing. The NUN is crying.)

BOY: It's from God alright, from God, only God could write a letter like that, only God is that educated, only God could say all that in a word, a word that hurts that much.

(The BOY looks at the letter then at the NUN. He throws the letter away, gets onto the bed and puts his arms around her.)

BOY: We both got it wrong. I thought he was dead, you thought he was good. He ain't dead, he just ain't what he's sold as, a dog of a God. A fucking great Doberman.

Act Two

SCENE ONE

(*BOY starts to recite 'The Owl and the Pussycat' to the NUN while holding her. The bed starts to suggest a boat. As he recites the poem the boy seduces the NUN, removing her wimple and then kissing her. There is a soundscape throughout this second act. It is important that the sound builds gradually in volume and in sense. It starts as a surreal sound which could be many things, the sea, prison sounds. In the storm scene it reaches a crescendo, after the blackout and silence the sound becomes very clearly that of prison and suggests that the noise before was this but warped.*

The bell rings and the soundscape starts to impinge on the BOY. He thinks it is coming from outside and gets excited. The suggestion of the boat stops. The BOY is listening by the door. He is getting excited. The bed still blocks the doorway.)

BOY: There's a fucking riot going on out there, a fucking riot! (*He starts to move the bed away from the door.*) A fucking riot!

NUN: What yon doyng?

(*The BOY ignores her and carries on trying to shift the bed. She sits on it to stop him. They are very close during the next argument.*)

NUN: What yon doyng?

BOY: There's a riot out there. We can tear this place apart, tear *Dread* apart.

NUN: Wynde thou not from this place!

BOY: Why not?

CROSSING THE BAR

NUN: Thybody beheld yond them gate, thybody seeyn vile thyngs.

(*The BOY suddenly remembers what he saw and hesitates.*)

BOY: It ain't like that anymore, what I hear ain't what I saw, it's different now.

NUN: Debate *Dread* from within or thy battle be lost, thereby nought yond them gate. *Dread* be within thyself, rente it from here, rage agaayn it from here.

BOY: How come you know so much?

NUN: Mybody hath ymaginacioun. A thynge thyn wolde hold of no value, them kepe it locked from you. What image can thy conjur? Your body be dead to wonder and magic. What vision be inthy lyfe? None, it be burrowed in shit. Thyn wolde hold no value to this magic of mind, yon glimpse no aungel on the road.

BOY: What's the point in pretend? That's kids' stuff.

NUN: Ymaginacioun be no false deyvse, it not be a thyng to shit out like a turd, it be what makes possible all thynges in all woldes. Noman espie Hevene with a glass or turn sulphur to gold unless ymaginacioun conjured first. Ymaginacioun be the fulcrum of lyfe. What sayn thou beyond that gate? What peyned you so?

BOY: Nothing, I saw nothing forever, forever nothing. Going on and on forever, just nothing. Hell is nothing.

NUN: *Dread* be within thyself, take battle with it here. You can't change thynges by dragging a manger or measure tyme with thy turds. But when yon body held me, ymagined my pain. Somethynge changed.

BOY: You felt it too?

CROSSING THE BAR

SCENE TWO

(*The NUN and the BOY are both back on the boat. They are sitting together looking out to sea.*)

BOY: The Owl and the Pussycat.

NUN: Adam and Eve.

BOY: Grant and Tiffany. Where to?

NUN: Matters not.

BOY: Somewhere.

NUN: Let the wind be beforn us.

BOY: Can you see anything?

NUN: Nought, mybody biholde nought.

BOY: Which way do we go?

NUN: This cours be forever. None to ask.

BOY: No-one.

NUN: Even not God.

BOY: Specially not him.

NUN: Just thee and thyn.

BOY: We can decide.

NUN: Biforn the wind?

BOY: Tack to either side.

(*NUN trails her hand in the sea.*)

BOY: We must be looking for something?

NUN: No.

BOY: Or it's looking for us. Maybe we'll smell it.

(*The ship starts to gather speed. BOY takes tiller to hold it.*)

CROSSING THE BAR

BOY: On a reach.

NUN: Wind push mybody. Carrying me on.

BOY: How long does it take?

NUN: This cours be eternal.

BOY: If this is forever, what shall we do?

NUN: Examine yon lyfe.

BOY: That won't take long.

NUN: Rummage yon soul.

BOY: Don't like the sound of that. (*He has spotted something.*) There, over there! I can see land. There's some land!

NUN: Thatbe the place of lyfe, of temporel thynges. Nought of our liken.

BOY: (*starting to change the direction of the ship*) Steer to its light.

NUN: (*trying to steer the boat back onto its old course*) Therebe marks on an edge, thym marks shewe death, thym lights fynde not us.

BOY: (*holding hard to the tiller*) Straight ahead.

NUN: Counsaile yon wind.

BOY: Sail against it.

NUN: (*still struggling with the BOY*) Thyn cours be marked out, surrender to death.

BOY: But if we see life?

NUN: Then why choyse yon to leve it?

BOY: There was nothing to hold me. We could just go and look. If we don't like it....

NUN: Resurrection be hard.

BOY: The distance is nothing.

CROSSING THE BAR

NUN: How deep a soul?

BOY: All I needed was someone. What the fuck's that?

(*The BOY is pointing at something in the sea.*)

NUN: It be a head, a head withhelde *Dread*, whose eyen chargeth somethyng. Surprised by death?

BOY: More likely by life.

NUN: Bereft of ymaginacioun.

BOY: A victim of choices.

NUN: Hym image marks displeasaunce.

BOY: Wouldn't you be?

NUN: And demaundes speke.

BOY: (*horrified*) Speak?

NUN: Behelde in hym eyen, humanite dispite.

BOY: S.O.S.

NUN: Speke clerely?

BOY: Save Our Souls.

NUN: Suffre me, pull it in.

BOY: We don't know where it's been.

(*BOY jumps out of the boat.*)

NUN: Cleve to me!

BOY: (*walking towards the head*) I'm walking on the water see, I'm walking on the water. Where has it gone? The head has gone under.

SCENE THREE

(*As the BOY messes around on the water, the KEEPER appears like a shadow carrying another candle. The BOY bumps into him and the 'boat' disappears.*)

CROSSING THE BAR

BOY: I'm drowning!

KEEPER: An accident?

(*The BOY looks at his trousers.*)

BOY: And there in a wood a Piggy-wig stood, with a ring on the end of his nose.

KEEPER: A thought.

(*The KEEPER goes to the candles and starts tending them as if making room for another.*)

BOY: It arrived to collect us, you never said.

KEEPER: Take me past that again.

BOY: You never said to expect it.

KEEPER: He's still due to arrive.

NUN: Thyn boat, hym spekes of a boat.

KEEPER: (*not understanding*) Good.

BOY: It was here.

KEEPER: Fancy.

BOY: Do you know where it takes us?

KEEPER: At a guess, where you like.

BOY: To the land. The land where the Bong tree grows.

KEEPER: Within reason.

BOY: (*goes to see what the KEEPER is doing*) What's that for?

KEEPER: The other, his soul arrived first.

BOY: Is he due for the journey?

KEEPER: From ashes to ashes.

BOY: No room on our ship.

KEEPER: His essence lacks substance. In advance of itself.

CROSSING THE BAR

	He jumped under a train, his head has gone AWOL.
NUN:	We behelde.
BOY:	A light.
NUN:	Hym head! Did float past us.
BOY:	A deadhead, pitched into the sea.
KEEPER:	(*sarcastically*) The Sea of Abandonment.
BOY:	Is that where we are?
KEEPER:	A metaphor, sonny, a metaphor for...
BOY:	...We've seen this 'met'.
KEEPER:	A very mediaeval thing to do.
NUN:	Imaged despair.
BOY:	Sad case.
KEEPER:	You all are. Committed to death. He relinquished his soul in advance, so expect....
BOY:	...We'll be gone.
KEEPER:	He'll notice if so.
BOY:	Gone over.
NUN:	But.
BOY:	Trust me.
KEEPER:	You taking the piss? Where are the fuck words, the boring, and the nothing? Where has this rhythm come from? Are you drifting towards a philosophy?
BOY:	Ever been on a ship?
KEEPER:	The Ship of Fools, the Ship of Death and the Ship of....
BOY:	...Tell the other he is welcome to *Dread*, we're leaving.

CROSSING THE BAR

KEEPER: I care for your souls, I've planted them deep.

BOY: Give them to others, we're travelling light.

NUN: We seke ferther out.

KEEPER: God?

NUN: Nought hym!

KEEPER: Your father?

NUN: Nought hym!

KEEPER: What's happened?

NUN: He's smelled some thyng.

BOY: God shit.

NUN: Somethyng sharp.

KEEPER: You travel as hollow shells without souls.

BOY: Good.

KEEPER: You're dangling with life.

BOY: We'll risk it.

KEEPER: What you plan is dangerous. To turn back now.

BOY: Even better.

KEEPER: There's a point in between the sea and the sky, Heaven and Hell, life and death. Where the debris of life carried out on the flow meets the sea and is forced to let go. If you fail to cross over that bar you go down with no soul.

BOY: The sea's full of souls, we'll catch one if need be. Piss off! We have other fish to fry.

(*The KEEPER picks up the discarded letter and opens and reads it.*)

KEEPER: I see you've been mentioned in dispatches.

(*He leaves, whistling. He takes the letter with him.*)

CROSSING THE BAR

SCENE FOUR

(*The NUN and BOY return to the boat.*)

BOY: Hard out, hard out!
NUN: Feel thy empty?
BOY: Full.
NUN: Mybody also.
BOY: So why did you ask?
NUN: Soulless marks empty.
BOY: Souls are like chains, they hold you down.
NUN: Some light our cours.
BOY: We can see by the other.
NUN: Hym light struggles weakly.
BOY: Obviously dodgy.
NUN: This merkness will lose us.
BOY: There's a light on the land.
NUN: What name holds this boat?
BOY: Words tell us nothing.
NUN: Inscribed by the side.

(*She leans over to look.*)

BOY: What does it matter?
NUN: Mybody be wondering.
BOY: Will it tell us how long?
NUN: (*as she reads*) "Dread nought".
BOY: Hold tight, going about!
NUN: Mybody hawks sik!
BOY: 'Course it don't.

CROSSING THE BAR

NUN: It do!

BOY: All them roaches.

(*She is sick. The boy sees it.*)

BOY: Disgusting! Them legs.

NUN: Now trewly I'm purged, nought beetles, nought soul. A vessel.

BOY: To fill?

NUN: You meaning?

BOY: Just a suggestion.

NUN: Twixt the jaws of death?

BOY: (*as he starts to remove his trousers*) A hung man dies ready. (*as he strokes her body*) I could fuck you for a year and a day.

NUN: What of tyme?

BOY: My need.

(*The NUN is looking at his neck.*)

NUN: Why words mark yon neck?

BOY: My mark.

NUN: (*She reads.*) "Cut Here".

BOY: My request to the world.

NUN: Happed thus?

BOY: Just gave me enough rope, and locked the door.

NUN: Why on yon body?

BOY: Tells the world where I stand. Takes the power away.

NUN: Christ was the lover mybody forswore.

BOY: I can walk on the water.

NUN: Hym carries marks in hym hands.

CROSSING THE BAR

BOY: Forget him, he's shacked up with Dot Cotton.

NUN: "Cut Here" be words?

BOY: Of despair.

NUN: My minde wonders, be our cours the image of each? Seke we the same?

BOY: How long will it take?

NUN: Tyme be in dispite.

BOY: I feel more alive.

NUN: That knowledge marks somethynge.

BOY: What?

NUN: What yon seke on thyn course.

(*He again starts to stroke her body.*)

BOY: Oh lovely pussy, my pussy, my love!

NUN: (*As she starts to back away from him.*) Yon cors be for one.

BOY: You ain't going without me!

NUN: It be not me departs, mybody sense somethyng, somethyng vital, a flame not snuffed out, a quickening of flesh.

BOY: Desire!

NUN: A body alive can not fuck the dead, yon quickening senses the bitters of lyfe. This sea be breathless sustaining the dead. Therebe storm rising up a passion for lyfe.

BOY: We can do it together.

NUN: Mybody lie with the dead and must swim with them souls, this crossing be yorn. My bloodlyfe be less, I will come to the edge, my shroud saile yon through.

(*Dark and windier. The NUN and BOY are struggling*

CROSSING THE BAR

to keep the ship under control as the storm comes up. The NUN is the mast and the sail. The BOY is at the tiller but is trying to get the NUN to take in the sail because of the rising storm.)

BOY: Get it straight! Get it straight!

NUN: Mysoule hurt!

BOY: Against the wind.

NUN: Wherebe?

BOY: Feel it.

NUN: It be allwhere?

BOY: Get it straight.

NUN: Myshroud chaffs in the wind.

BOY: Just look for a heading.

NUN: My ears here thyn chains, thyn chains of thyn souls.

(They struggle against the storm.)

BOY: Just do what you're doing, point the wind.

NUN: Nay wiste be thyn wind, this hasard forby.

BOY: Steer with your body.

NUN: Would mybody steer my soul.

BOY: Too late for that.

NUN: This be harrowing of Hell!

BOY: Don't look.

NUN: Lips of thyn dead curl over the bow.

BOY: Straight ahead, don't look!

NUN: At those pointing dead.

BOY: Look just in front. Be brave! I've seen Hell. And nothing is as terrible as nothing.

CROSSING THE BAR

(*The NUN gets off the bed and crouches in the same corner in which she started the play.*)

BOY: If I'm smashed at the bar?

NUN: Death then embrace yon as cadivar bride.
(*The BOY sails on to cross the bar.*)

BOY: Tell deadhead he should have missed the train, not the point.
(*The storm gets worse.*)

BOY: Knuckled courage bare, buck naked.
Sucking and spewing sinews of souls,
As the dead sea closes over me.
I cross the bar.
Bloody bones breaking breathless bodies.
Chainstokes the seabed.
As the dead lie dead.
I cross the bar.

(*He looks at the broken rope [still hanging from the ceiling] as if looking at this own body, then he takes off his shirt.*)

BOY: Dangling.
Naked before death.
A twisting, buckling body in its contorted death.
Dancing on nothing.
Committed to life by a thread.
Full blood ears clog, the pulsing deathsong.
As the strains of life fight back.
Against the executioners death roll my heart beats for its life.
Grasped with two bare naked hands, knuckles
                raw from the fight,
Hands weathered with courage.
Salt stung with death but still quick with its
                blood.
I cross the bar.
Launched towards life.
Alive is everything.

CROSSING THE BAR

    Death before time, nothing.
    I've looked into hell and nothing is as terrible
                                          as nothing.
    So chart into the wind!
    Buck naked to the pointing dead.
    Hard out! Hard out!
    Unfurl the souls.
    Chart the winds.
    Pitch and yaw.
    I'm crossing the bar!

(The storm reaches a crescendo as he clings onto the boat. Black out as he crosses the bar.)

SCENE FIVE

(Silence. The NUN is holding the BOY up to the rope. [The image has resonances of the descent from the cross.] Bright light and loud alarm bell at the same time, light and sound like an explosion. The GAOLER enters having seen the BOY hanging through the door peephole and has set off the alarm. He 'cuts' the BOY down, the NUN drops him. The GAOLER removes the noose. After a silence it becomes clear that the BOY is alive as he starts gasping for breath. The sounds of the prison are now clear. The GAOLER is carrying a letter.)

GAOLER: That's it laddy, that's it, let it back in.

        (The BOY vomits in the same place the NUN did earlier.)

GAOLER: The stuff of life.

        (The BOY looks at his vomit.)

BOY: No legs.

GAOLER: Bin dangling too long.

CROSSING THE BAR

BOY: I'm alive?

GAOLER: Only just, what game were you playing? If you'd bin wearing stockings I'd have said you were turning yourself on! (*said with relish*) Auto-erotica, nice word that. But your politics ain't right, so what was your game? Turning off.

BOY: Called *Dread*.

GAOLER: Sounds like graffiti, or a dangerous game.

BOY: I'll not play it again.

(*The GAOLER hands him the letter but the BOY draws back from it.*)

GAOLER: You'd have missed this.

BOY: She weren't going to write.

GAOLER: Everyone's entitled to a change of heart.

(*The BOY takes the letter.*)

THE END

Head

Head was commissioned and broadcast by BBC Radio 4 on 29th October, 1996.

CHARACTERS

ISABELLA (ELLA)
Liza Sadovy
ENZO/THE HEAD
Tom Hollander
WOLFSKIN/(ELLA'S BROTHER)
Sean Baker
THE POET (A CONFUSED ROMANTIC POET)
Mark Bonnar

Directed by   Jonquil Panting

Act One
SCENE ONE

(*The action of the play takes place in the POET'S garret in a flat in a high rise block. There is no particular time-set but outside in the passageways and stairwells lurk packs of half-animal cannibal beggars.*
   The POET is writing using a scratchy quill pen. He sits in a small but comfortable garret room with a crackling fire for warmth and a candle for light. There is the occasional sound of a fly buzzing.)

POET: (*writing*) ...Sick and wan
The brothers' faces in the ford did seem,
Lorenzo's flush with love.... They'd pass'd the
                                  water
Into a forest quiet for the slaughter.
There was Lorenzo slain and buried in....

(*A fly buzzes irritatingly, POET tries to swot it.*)

(*Swot.*)

Go buzz somewhere else.

(*writing*)

There in that forest did his great love cease....

(*The fly continues to buzz.*)

POET: (*writing*) It was a vision. ...In the drowsy gloom,
The dull of midnight, at her couch's foot
Lorenzo stood, and wept: the forest tomb....
Strange sound it was, when the pale shadow
                                  spoke....

HEAD

(*fly buzz*)

(*The sound of the fly gets nearer and nearer as if to land on the POET'S nose.*)

SCENE TWO

(*ELLA'S bedroom. ELLA is crying.*)

GHOST: Isabella.... Isabella.... Isabella....

(*ELLA stops crying.*)

Isabella....

(*slowly*)

Don't be afraid.

ELLA: (*whispers urgently*) Enzo?

GHOST: I am here.

ELLA: Where?

GHOST: At the foot of your bed....

ELLA: Enzo!

GHOST: (*slowly as she looks at him*) Don't be afraid.

ELLA: (*intake of breath*) Why are you so... pale? So... undone? How did you get here? Where have you been? I've been waiting... you....

GHOST: (*interrupts*) Your grief heaved me from the grave.

ELLA: Grave?

GHOST: (*continuing*) Stalked my death. I....

ELLA: Death?

GHOST: (*indignantly*) You wail so much!

ELLA: I didn't know where you were.... You just left without.... (*retort*) Why didn't you phone?

HEAD

GHOST: I wasn't watching for death.... Murder has no symptoms!

ELLA: (*shocked*) Murder!

GHOST: Your brother.

ELLA: Wolfskin?

GHOST: Through the heart.... It's not only his body he likes piercing.... And now your grief shatters my death.

ELLA: Your death? When you left I was.... Wolfskin said.... (*cries out*) Hold me!

GHOST: I cannot, this image is transient.

ELLA: What do you mean?

GHOST: I lie underleaf, earthbound.

ELLA: (*desperate*) If you love me don't torment me with riddles!

GHOST: Come find my deathplace. Ella, cool it with tears. My burying was done in disguise. Mark my mortsafe with this grief which rocks life, mark it forever. Lay your grief in the ground, weep over me and then move on.

ELLA: How will I find you?

GHOST: The forest holds my boneseed.

ELLA: I will find you, Enzo. I will find you!

GHOST: I return to my hiding place.

ELLA: My eyes are covered, go quickly.... (*she counts*) ONE TWO THREE FOUR FIVE SIX SEVEN EIGHT NINE TEN.

(*ELLA gets up and runs towards the door.*)

ELLA: Even if you've fallen off the earth.... I'll find your carcass.... I'll tell it I love it, wrap it in softness, hold your smell to my heart. Coming to find you, ready or not.

HEAD

(*ELLA opens the door.*)

BROTHER: (*suddenly, loudly and firmly*) Where are you going?

ELLA: (*startled*) I....

(*She tries to get past him.*)

BROTHER: (*stops her*) You can't go out there.

ELLA: I want to find him. My lover....

BROTHER: I told you he's gone off with a floozy.

ELLA: He told me you'd... you'd....

BROTHER: What? What did he tell you?

ELLA: (*changes her mind*) That he loved me....

BROTHER: He had that wandering man glint.

ELLA: You hurt me.

BROTHER: He's gone.... Bury his memory deep.

ELLA: I need something to bury! Memory's too cheap.

BROTHER: It's dangerous out there.... The lift might get stuck, the beggars will eat you. You are safe here.

ELLA: If I look out on the balcony.

BROTHER: I've told you before, you must stay back.

ELLA: I feel like a princess in a tower.

BROTHER: (*laughs*) Go to bed Sleeping Beauty, brother Wolfskin will look after you.

ELLA: He didn't say goodbye.

BROTHER: (*firmly*) Go to bed.

SCENE TWO (a)

(*The garret. The POET is writing with his scratchy quill.*)

POET: When the full morning came, she had devised
How she might secret to the forest hie;
How she might find the clay, so dearly prized,
And sing it one last lullaby....

SCENE THREE

(A forest. ELLA is running through the trees. She is breathing fast. Occasionally she laughs hysterically then runs a bit further, pushing her way through undergrowth, snapping branches, etc.)

ELLA: *(said in a sing-song way, with a touch of hysteria)*

Coming to find you, ready or not!

(silence)

Coming to find you, ready or not!

(silence)

(She runs further through the forest, laughing hysterically.)

Coming to find you!

(She stops, breathless.)

Am I warm?

(silence)

(shouts) I said.... Am I warm?

ELLA: *(crossly)* Damn you! ...Am I warm?

(Silence. She runs on further, then wades through a river, as she wades she says —)

ELLA: If I pull back these sheets, will I trawl your soul up from the deep?

(She climbs up the bank. She is dripping wet and breathless.)

HEAD

ELLA: (*despairingly*) Why do you hide from me?

(*silence*)

ELLA: I love you!

(*She cups her hands and shouts.*)

ELLA: I love you... love you, love you, love you....
(*desperate*) Give me a clue.... Anything.... A sign....
I've read that shallow graves are marked by corpse candles.

(*She breaks twigs as she moves on. She falls and cries out.*)

ELLA: My body treads this landscape hunting your death.... I will not give up.... Believe me, I will not give up....

(*The fly buzzes.*)

(*She laughs triumphantly.*)

ELLA: A fly!

(*laughs*)

ELLA: A fly marks your mortsafe! I find you! You can come out now.... I find you.... I know you're under there.

(*She jumps onto an earth mound.*)

ELLA: Under there.... Under there.... You can come out now.

(*There is a long silence. Her tone changes, determined.*)

ELLA: Alright then, I'll dig you out! No earthbarrow holds you for long.... Only I can hold you.... Hiding from me.... Under there!

(*She starts to dig. The fly buzzes.*)

ELLA: I dig. Clawgritfull pain ache. On the hearth of your death. (*pause*) Hardly daring to step in.

(*She starts to dig with her hands, more and more*

HEAD

frantically. She digs like a dog, panting and crying out occasionally. Sound of earth flying through the air until she reaches LORENZO'S body. She cries out as she pulls out a hand.)

ELLA: (*slowly getting faster*)
Coldsweat hand on body,
This is not you, Enzo,
This is not you....
Smell-less stench fleshgone,
Face teethbone hair,
Earthfull blood quickstill,
Freshlydead flesh.
This is not you, Enzo!

(*pause*)

(*fly buzz*)

ELLA: Home,
Take you home,
By the hearth of my life,
Raise, dead up again!

(*She starts to try and pull the body out of the grave.*)

ELLA: Pull you up!

(*As she pulls.*)

ELLA: Heave, heave homeward this body,
Heave it homeward....

(*As she pulls.*)

ELLA: Heave, Heave!

(*having difficulty*)

ELLA: Heave.

(*She gives up.*)

ELLA: Death is too heavy to heave from the grave.
I will climb in there with you.
Perching a precipice your death spinning below
             me.

HEAD

ELLA: Carry me, Enzo,
Into the home of the grave.

(*She climbs in.*)

ELLA: Cover me over,
Fill my blood with this earth.

(*She lies down. Long silence.*)

(*Fly buzzes.*)

ELLA: This barrow has no depth,
Holds barely even you.

(*Silence. Fly buzzes.*)

ELLA: My sleep will not rest here.

(*She climbs out. Fly buzzes.*)

ELLA: If I can't carry all.
Your head holds an imprint.
The pitch of the face.
The shaft of the hair.
If I hack helldown.
Haul your head heavenward.

(*She starts to hack off the head with great difficulty using a blunt knive. As she hacks —*)

ELLA: Helldown.

(*as she pulls at head*)

ELLA: Heavenward.

(*as she hacks*)

ELLA: Helldown....

(*as she pulls*)

ELLA: Heavenward....

(*sawing*)

ELLA: I will take you home, Enzo....

HEAD

	A trophy of love. You head holds my grief. (*The fly is buzzing frantically now around the head. As she hacks one final blow the head is severed.*)
ELLA:	One final blow your head leaves its body.
HEAD:	Theda detha dathe thaedeath....
ELLA:	Has a soul taken flight?
HEAD:	Detha, theda, dathe, deathhead.
ELLA:	Enzo?
HEAD:	Deathhead. Put back to my body. Put back to the ground. (*Fly buzzes.*)
ELLA:	Enzo?
HEAD:	Back to my body.... Back to the ground....

SCENE THREE (a)

(*The POET is writing with his scratchy quill.*)

POET:	If Love impersonate was ever dead, Pale Isabella kiss'd it, and low, moaned. 'Twas love; cold.... Dead indeed, but not de-throned....

SCENE FOUR

(*By a stream. ELLA is bathing the HEAD.*)

ELLA:	(*As she bathes the HEAD.*) You are still Enzo.
HEAD:	Dead Enzo.
ELLA:	My Enzo, the flesh is just....
HEAD:	Be truthful.

HEAD

ELLA: Falling off. But the set of the jaw, the bridge of the nose, it is you, I can see you and hold you.

HEAD: (*irony*) In the palm of your hand.

ELLA: It's enough.

HEAD: Hold me to water, show me.

ELLA: Best not.

HEAD: Show me. Let me see what you're seeing.

ELLA: First I'll bathe your eye sockets, pick the earth from your teeth, repair you a little, the flesh will stick on.

HEAD: (*persistently*) Show me.

ELLA: (*holds his head over the stream*) There see, it is you.

HEAD: (*shocked*) My eye sockets are wormy, the flesh livid and green.

ELLA: I like the colour, it's....

HEAD: (*distressed*) This is death Ella, wormy and earthful, my hair!

ELLA: I can unravel that.

HEAD: Ouch!

ELLA: It's tangled. I'll soon find your curls.

HEAD: Feed me back to the ground.

ELLA: No! (*as she continues to comb his hair*) Do you remember how I played with your hair?

HEAD: Called me Goldilocks....

ELLA: ...And nibbled your ears.

HEAD: This will not do. Death is a different game.

ELLA: Then why did you call me?

HEAD: I thought if I showed you the mound, let your tears fall griefground, you could move on. I didn't

HEAD

	expect you to dig up my corpse and hack off my head.
ELLA:	Grief doesn't melt like ice at the burial. It climbs in the grave and moulders around gathering details.
HEAD:	But my head!
ELLA:	Holds my grief.
HEAD:	Not in a bag!

SCENE 4 (a)

(*The garret. The POET is writing with his scratchy quill.*)

POET: In anxious secrecy they took it home,
And then the prize was all for Isabel....

SCENE FIVE

(*Inside a lift that goes up to nearly the top of the high-rise flat. As the lift goes up it makes a rhythmic clunking noise as it reaches each floor. But it doesn't stop. ELLA is in the lift breathing deeply because she is nervous. The fly buzzes.*)

POET:	These lifts are not pleasant.
ELLA:	No.
POET:	Are you alright?
ELLA:	Yes.
POET:	You look ruffled.
ELLA:	Like a bird?
POET:	Covered in mud.

HEAD

ELLA: I've been digging.

POET: Shall I carry your shopping?

ELLA: (*alarmed*) No!

POET: You live just below me.

ELLA: Yes.

POET: You come out so seldom.

ELLA: Seldom.

POET: Isabella.

ELLA: You know my name?

POET: From the poem....

ELLA: Ella for short.

POET: You live with your brother....

ELLA: He likes killing things.

POET: And piercing his body.... He looks stapled together, his hair razor sharp.... He mustn't find the head.

ELLA: What?

POET: In the bag.... He musn't find it.

ELLA: Ho... how did you know?

POET: Hide it well.

ELLA: Who are you?

POET: A poet.... (*The lift stops.*) This is your floor?

ELLA: Yes.

POET: (*The doors open.*) See you again.

(*ELLA leaves. The lift continues on up.*)

HEAD

SCENE SIX

(ELLA walks into the flat. Her BROTHER appears suddenly and startles her.)

BROTHER: Where have you been? Mud! What's all this mud? How did you get out? What have you there?

ELLA: (*quickly*) Mushrooms!

BROTHER: What?

ELLA: For your breakfast.

BROTHER: That big?

ELLA: It's a puffball.

BROTHER: What's that smell?

ELLA: Puffballs are earthy.

BROTHER: Cook while I shave.... I'll have devil's kidneys with that fungus.

(He leaves the room. ELLA goes into the kitchen.)

HEAD: You called me a puffball?

ELLA: SSHHH!

HEAD: But a puffball.

ELLA: SSHHH! He will hear you.

(She opens the fridge door.)

HEAD: Not in there!

ELLA: He won't find you.

(ELLA slams the fridge door shut then starts to cook breakfast, frying kidneys and chopping mushrooms. BROTHER comes back. The fridge has started to make a chattering noise.)

BROTHER: Don't leave here again.

ELLA: I need to go out, Brother. I go mad here talking to people.

BROTHER: There's no-one here.
ELLA: People.... I imagine....
BROTHER: Like who?
ELLA: Poets.
BROTHER: What's wrong with the fridge?
ELLA: (*She kicks it.*) It does that sometimes.
BROTHER: It sounds like teeth....
ELLA: (*gives BROTHER breakfast*) Could be pigs' chaps. Can't I go out today?
BROTHER: When I find you a husband. This isn't puffball!
ELLA: I'm saving that for something special.
BROTHER: There's a cartfull of rich men coming to town, if you're not too earthy one of them might like you.
ELLA: Is that why you killed him?
BROTHER: What did you say?
ELLA: (*quickly changes her mind*) I said I feel ill, don't go out tonight, Brother. I'll cook you the puffball.
BROTHER: I've heard of a new beggarpack on the edge.... (*significantly*) I shall go and fleece them.... Don't leave the flat, I may bring home a richman.

(*The BROTHER leaves.*)

SCENE SIX (a)

(*The garret. The POET writing with a scratchy quill.*)

POET: She calmed its wild hair with a golden comb,
And all around each eye's sepulchral cell
Pointed each fringed lash; the smeared loam
With tears, as chilly as a dripping well....

HEAD

SCENE SEVEN

(*The flat. ELLA takes the now frozen HEAD out of the fridge. Its teeth are chattering. The fly is buzzing around.*)

HEAD: It's freezing in there.

ELLA: Ripe for resurrection!

HEAD: I am dead, Ella.... My flesh is undone, my hair matted with death....

ELLA: (*The fly buzzes, ELLA swots at it.*) If I could roll back the tombstone....

HEAD: That's an old story, it doesn't work anymore.

ELLA: (*to HEAD*) I shall braid your hair... like a warrior.

(*ELLA starts to comb his hair.*)

ELLA: On the battlefields they hacked off the heads and braided the hair.

HEAD: You should have left me underearth....

ELLA: I missed you.... I'll wrap you in silk... tie gold ribbons in your hair.

HEAD: Take me back to the forest.

ELLA: (*as she braids his hair*)

There's a beauty in death's raggedness,
The edge of the flesh
The bone showing through,
With these flashes of gold,
And the white of your teeth.

HEAD: Let my head feed the ground.

ELLA: I love you so much my heart bursts.... (*as she finishes braiding*) There... now you look... (*pause as she thinks of word*) Wholesome! (*sprays the HEAD with hairspray*)

HEAD: (*starts to cough*) What are you doing now?!
ELLA: I want you to smell like you used to, that sweet smell of love.
HEAD: This is the odour of death.
ELLA: If I coat you in hairspray, glue the flesh back on, it's almost....
HEAD: (*interrupts, annoyed*) I feel like a Cindy doll.
ELLA: (*angry*) You are so selfish! You die without telling me, and then you whine to be buried. Did you ever love me? Why can't I keep you?
HEAD: (*slightly whiny*) I need to be buried, where the maggots will flourish, be in the earth to moulder away.
ELLA: (*petulant*) This is a tenement flat, I haven't got any earth.
HEAD: (*quoting dictionary*) Death is the cessation of life!
ELLA: You used to talk of love, now it's only of death.
HEAD: (*fly buzzing around*) My language has changed like my smell.
ELLA: While I carry you close I can cope with this death thing. Letting go is hard. (*swots the fly*) (*to fly*) Go plague someone else.
HEAD: He paces my corridors sucking up sinews.
ELLA: (*disgusted*) I don't want to know that!
HEAD: Then bury me! Hide death under the ground. Make your memory my tomb, hold me in there.
ELLA: I want to cheat death, cling to your image.
HEAD: I'm just an earth ball.... Turn your grief to revenge. Make me into a brainball to hurl at your brother.
ELLA: (*cross*) Or cook your brains for his dinner.
HEAD: If you do that he takes on my strength.

HEAD

HEAD: If you do that he takes on my strength.

ELLA: Then I'll just give him lamb's liver and onions. (*She starts chopping onions. The doorbell goes. ELLA answers the door.*)

POET: I....

ELLA: The poet!

POET: We need to talk.

ELLA: I'm cooking dinner.

POET: I've brought you a present. (*He hands her a pot of basil.*)

ELLA: (*She takes it, puzzled.*) A basil plant?

POET: It's a pot of basil.... (*explanation*) You can bury the head in it.

ELLA: I keep that in the fridge.

POET: This will be better.

ELLA: It'll smell.

POET: Heads do.

ELLA: I don't like the smell, it's not Enzo.

POET: (*firmly*) You can bury it here.

ELLA: But I want to bathe him and keep him.

POET: (*trying to be forceful*) Put the head in here. (*as he pulls the plant out of the pot*) If I pull out the plant, see the earth begs for a head.

ELLA: But it's dirty, earth will fill up his eye sockets.

POET: (*getting a bit desperate*) Please put the head in the pot. You're losing the script.

HEAD: If you loved me.

ELLA: But.... (*searching for an excuse*) There's a crack in the pot!

HEAD

HEAD: I'll peep through it, catch glimpses of you.

ELLA: Are you in this together?

POET: It's the drift of the poem, you put the head in the pot.

HEAD: I cry out to be buried.

ELLA: (*puts the HEAD in the pot*) I'll cover you over but not very deep. (*as she covers him over*) Keep your eye to the crack.

POET: (*relieved*) We're now back on track, the poem is flowing.

ELLA: (*places the pot on the mantlepiece*) I'll put him here. (*matter-of-fact*) So what happens now?

POET: (*hesitates*) Wait and see.

ELLA: I want to know where I'm going, how all this ends.

POET: You fade away....

ELLA: (*can't believe what she's heard*) Sorry?

POET: You fade away in a madness of grief.

ELLA: After all that I've done?!

POET: When your brother finds the head... he takes it away and....

ELLA: (*interrupts*) What sort of poem is this?

POET: A romance.

ELLA: Haven't you heard of revenge? (*sound of lift outside*) Wolfskin! Home for his dinner. (*teasing*) I should feed him poet.

POET: He can't see me.

ELLA: If he catches a whiff.

POET: Poet's don't smell.

ELLA: If I fried you with onions then the story would change.

POET: (*The door is being unlocked.*) You can't change the story.

ELLA: (*resolute*) But I don't want to fade away.

SCENE EIGHT

(*In the flat. The fly is buzzing around. The BROTHER enters. ELLA is chopping onions.*)

BROTHER: Someone's pissed in the lift again.

ELLA: There's blood on your leg.

BROTHER: The beggars bit me.

ELLA: If you will kick them.

BROTHER: They wouldn't give me their money.

ELLA: (*starts frying liver, sound of sizzling*) They have to live.

BROTHER: No they don't! Dead is what all beggars should be. (*sniffs*) What's cooking?

ELLA: Liver and onions....

(*The fly is buzzing around the basil plant pot.*)

HEAD: (*blowing at fly*) Not now! I can't hear what they're saying.

BROTHER: Bought a load off a wagon cheap, make a mint on it. Where's all this earth come from?

ELLA: A basil plant. I'll fetch the broom.

BROTHER: Are you turning that balcony into a garden? I told you nature is dirty, we don't need it.

ELLA: The plant's in a pot. I use it in cooking.... It's good for headaches. There's a poem about it....

HEAD

POET: (*to himself*) My poem.

BROTHER: Why do you bother with such stuff?

ELLA: It's so close to life....

BROTHER: You don't know what life is!

ELLA: It's about a woman whose lover was killed by her brother....

BROTHER: Boring.

ELLA: It used to be a romance.

POET: (*puzzled*) What does she mean, used to be?

BROTHER: That fly likes your basil.

ELLA: It's the smell.

BROTHER: It's found a crack in the pot. I'll get the fly spray.

ELLA: No! Your dinner is ready.

HEAD: (*blowing at fly*) Leave me alone!

BROTHER: It's gone right inside... (*He goes over to the plant and peers into the crack. His voice is heard within the pot.*) The smell!

HEAD: (*referring to the BROTHER, who doesn't hear him*) Uggh! Your breath does!

ELLA: The liver's a bit off.

BROTHER: (*still sniffing the pot*) It's coming from the pot... not like basil. What's in here?

ELLA: Nothing! Don't do that! You're making a mess! Stop that!

BROTHER: (*pulls HEAD out*) I think... I think it's a head!

ELLA: You're imagining things!

BROTHER: No, I'm not.... It's a head.

POET: (*excited*) It's the moment I told her about.... The jeopardy's set.

HEAD

ELLA: It's just roots.

BROTHER: I can see eye sockets.

ELLA: The bulb.

BROTHER: That's hair... I can feel... teeth! Who is it?

ELLA: You should know that!

BROTHER: A head bleeding mud.... Who?

ELLA: Come on Brother, you should know who this is. Don't those hollow eyes tell you something?

BROTHER: What are all these bits... of ribbon?

ELLA: (*snatches the HEAD and holds it up to show him*)

ELLA: Look at the flesh, those curls? Who does this look like nuzzling my ear?

BROTHER: Lorenzo!

ELLA: Bingo!

POET: (*puzzled, worried*) She's being a bit assertive.

BROTHER: Where did you get this?

ELLA: Where you left it.

BROTHER: (*fierce*) Give it to me.

POET: That's right, take it, take it from her.

ELLA: No, I'm keeping it.

POET: You can't!

BROTHER: You can't.

ELLA: Says who?

POET: I do!

BROTHER: I do!

ELLA: (*baiting him*) Come and get it.

POET: What is she doing?

HEAD

BROTHER: I will.

(*The BROTHER runs at ELLA.*)

POET: Go for it!!

ELLA: (*moves out of the way*) Missed!

BROTHER: (*dives at her again and gets hold of the HEAD and pulls at it*) Let go!

ELLA: (*as she stuggles with the head*) Never!

BROTHER: (*triumphant*) I have a chunk of his hair. (*horrified*) His skin crumbles!

ELLA: It's death. May it stick to you.

BROTHER: (*makes a dive at the HEAD and gets it*) Got it!

ELLA: (*very fierce*) Give it back!

BROTHER: (*teasing her*) I think the beggars would like this.

ELLA: Give it back to me!

POET: (*relieved*) Now the fading begins.

ELLA: (*She picks up the frying pan and charges at BROTHER.*) Give me back Enzo. Give me back that head!

(*She hits him over the head with the heavy frying pan. The BROTHER falls down and drops the HEAD.*)

(*silence*)

SCENE NINE

(*In the flat.*)

POET: (*flapping*) You weren't supposed to do that. Women are so unruly!

ELLA: (*looking at her BROTHER*) His wolfskin comes off.

POET: Is he dead?

HEAD

ELLA: (*as she inspects the BROTHER*) He's all soft inside. Like a lamb.

POET: What do we do with the body?

HEAD: Hack off the head.

POET: One head is enough.

ELLA: Put it in the lift.

POET: But someone will find it!

ELLA: The beggars will eat it.

HEAD: Cannibalism!

POET: But the theme was decay!

ELLA: We'll put him outside. Help me.

POET: (*trying to lift the BROTHER*) I can't lift him up. He's too heavy.

ELLA: The dead are. (*THE POET helps to pull the BROTHER'S body.*) Drag him... open the door.

POET: (*as he pulls body*) This is so....

ELLA: Modern?

(*They push the body outside and shut the door.*)

POET: (*breathless*) Now what do we do? (*to himself, thinking aloud*) If you talk to yourself, hold the festering head as your grief.

ELLA: (*scornfully*) Sounds boring! My grief has moved on.

POET: (*getting desperate*) I'm following a story, a traditional one, Boccaccio. A master.

ELLA: Did he write about the tenement and this piss stinking lift?

POET: Updates.... It's the contemporary theme.

ELLA: A highrise?

HEAD

POET: They are very indicative. Heaven and Hell.

HEAD: What about limbo.

ELLA: I'd forgotten about you.

HEAD: Make me the focus!

POET: You!

HEAD: Call it 'The Head'. Place me somewhere high up!

ELLA: (*mischievously*) The fridge.

HEAD: No! On the hat stand that's high up. Make it a scaffold, stand it out on the balcony. Let the crows take my flesh, pick me clean.

ELLA: There's not much left to pick.

POET: (*fed up*) He's just a skull! And my poem is picked clean.

(*The BROTHER starts hammering on the door.*)

BROTHER: (*from outside, sounding sheeplike, bleating*) Let me in! Let me in!

POET: He's not dead! This isn't even revenge.

ELLA: (to POET) 'Revenge is a dish best eaten cold.' (*shouting to BROTHER*) No brother Wolfskin! This is my tower now, go hunt with the beggars.

BROTHER: (*bleating*) Let me in... they will eat me... let me in.

ELLA: (*mischievously*) Not by the hair on my chinny chin chin....

BROTHER: (*bleating*) Please let me in.... (*His words turn into unidentifiable bleating.*)

POET: (*desperate*) What does all this mean?

ELLA: That the story has changed. I'll wrap the head in his wolfskin and take it back to the forest, back to the ground.

POET: What of your grief?

HEAD

ELLA: That will perch like a bird in my memory, ready to swoop at unguarded moments. (*as she wraps the HEAD in the wolfskin*) It is soft in here, Enzo. I'll wrap you in fur like a baby; my love holds your head. I will take you underground. (*to the POET*) Go write how strength grows out of grief, the way it springs up like a shoot from despair and decay. Write about that!

SCENE TEN

(*The garret. The POET typing on a computer. In the background the sound of the lift descending.*)

POET: (*typing*)
She descended in the lift,
To the heart of the forest,
The shaft of her lover's death was filled with
                                                  his head.
As she buried her grief....

(*Fade out on sound of fly buzzing.*)

THE END

Our Lady of Shadows

Our Lady of Shadows is a radio play. It was recorded in June 1994 by BBC Radio 3 with the following cast for broadcast as a Studio 3 production.

CHARACTERS

CATHERINE: The Lady of Shalott
Claire Skinner

KNIGHT: Sir Launcelot
Malcolm Ward

VOICE & HAG
Tessa Worsley

SHADOW (silent)

SISTER IGNATIOUS: An elderly nun
Rosemary Leach

Directed by Richard Wortley

This play has been written because it is time the Lady of Shalott was released.

Act One
SCENE ONE

(This is not a naturalistic play. It is a dramatic poem controlled by rhythms. The setting is a room in a tower in the middle ages. It is very dark, only the ephemeral light from the reflected images of a camera obscura shines upon the floor. The four verses of the Tennyson poem, "The Lady of Shalott", used in the play are read by someone other than CATHERINE.)

(first verse of Tennyson's poem)

VOICE: On either side the river lie
Long fields of barley and of rye,
That clothe the world and meet the sky:

(sound of nuns chanting underneath poem)

And thro' the field the road runs by
To many towered Camelot:
And up and down the people go,
Gazing where the lilies blow
Round an island here below,
The island of Shalott.

(The sound of nuns chanting a plainsong at Compline continues for a while after the verse ends. Then there is a loud explosion.)

OUR LADY OF SHADOWS

SCENE TWO

"The Shallop flitteth silken sailed"

(*In this scene CATHERINE is fifteen years old. The sound of a boat being rowed and, in the distance, nuns singing the mass of the dead. Also, sounds from the adjacent village. CATHERINE and SISTER IGNATIOUS are in the rowing boat heading for the island. SISTER IGNATIOUS is rowing and finding it hard going.*)

(*second verse of poem*)
(*sound of rowing is heard underneath verse*)

VOICE: Willows whiten apsens quiver,
Little breezes dusk and shiver
Thro' the wave that runs forever
By the island in the river
Flowing down to Camelot.
Four grey walls and four grey towers,
Overlook a space of flowers,
And the silent Isle embowers
The Lady of Shalott.

CATHERINE: Sister Iggy.

SISTER IGN.: Yes, child.

CATHERINE: Why sing they the mass of the dead?

SISTER IGN.: For you.

CATHERINE: Will you drown me?

SISTER IGN.: In solitude.

CATHERINE: Will it pain me?

SISTER IGN.: Poor child.

CATHERINE: Will you tell me why?

SISTER IGN.: Some thought you had conjured the devil.

OUR LADY OF SHADOWS

CATHERINE: 'Twas only the ochre of sulphur.
SISTER IGN.: Some thought they would die.
CATHERINE: The fire went out quickly!
SISTER IGN.: But you do such dangerous things.
CATHERINE: To find the secrets of the world.
SISTER IGN.: God's magic is sacred.
CATHERINE: But if I'd made gold!
SISTER IGN.: You go too far.
CATHERINE: There is far to go.
SISTER IGN.: Not now.

(*They land on the island and pull up the boat. They walk to the retreat tower and then start to climb the stone spiral stairs to the top of the tower.*)

CATHERINE: I am to retreat?
SISTER IGN.: Holy Mother thought it best.
CATHERINE: For how long?
SISTER IGN.: Your life.
CATHERINE: Will I die of starvation?
SISTER IGN.: No, in natural time. (*stops briefly as she is out of breath*) Food will be brought to you.
CATHERINE: But what am I to do?
SISTER IGN.: I have here your colours and vellum, practise your skill, devote your life to illuminating God's word.
CATHERINE: Why seal me up?
SISTER IGN.: We promised your father.
CATHERINE: Promised him what?
SISTER IGN.: To keep you safe, and chaste.

OUR LADY OF SHADOWS

(*They reach the door of the cell.*)

CATHERINE: But to be locked away.

SISTER IGN.: We did not know what else to do with you.

(*SISTER IGNATIOUS puts all CATHERINE'S things in the cell.*)

SISTER IGN.: You grow out of our care.

CATHERINE: Could not you just let me go?

SISTER IGN.: Take this. (*She hands her a lens.*)

CATHERINE: My lens.

SISTER IGN.: I saved it from the fire, I know you treasure it. Though why anyone should want to see things further or bigger than God intended makes no sense to me.

(*The door is locked and all outside sounds disappear.*)

CATHERINE: It is small and dark in here.

SCENE THREE

"Up and down the people go"

(*CATHERINE is pacing her tower as the third and fourth verses of the poem are read. Underneath each of the verses CATHERINE says her speeches.*)

(*poem*)

VOICE: By the margin, willow veil'd,
Slide the heavy barges trail'd
By slow horses; and unhail'd
Skimming down to Camelot:
But who hath seen her wave her hand?
Or at the casement seen her stand?
Or is she known in all the land,
The Lady of Shalott?

OUR LADY OF SHADOWS

CATHERINE: (*pacing*)

    I walk round and round,
    Round and round,
    Shadowing the world.
    God in her tower.
    I walk round and round,
    Round and round.
    Knowledge lines my walls.
    Gold-leaf saints litter the floor.

    (*poem*)

VOICE: Only reapers, reaping early
    In among the bearded barley,
    Hear a song that echoes cheerly
    From the river winding clearly,
    Down to towered Camelot:
    And by the moon the reaper weary,
    Piling sheaves in uplands airy,
    Listening, whispers "'Tis the fairy
    Lady of Shalott".

CATHERINE: (*Pacing. During this verse a thwacking sound starts to be heard which continues into the next scene.*)

    I walk round and round,
    Following my shadow around the room,
    Charting time like a ship on the sea.
    I walk round and round,
    A darkened chamber.
    Imitating people playing out their lives.
    My anchor straining on the tide of ritual.

SCENE FOUR

"Gazing where the lilies blow"

(*CATHERINE is walking around the camera obscura swatting at the figure of the HAG in the image.*)

CATHERINE: (*thwack*)

I've squashed her again!

(*thwack*)

Again! As flat as a flounder.

(*thwack*)

And again!

(*She scratches a notch on the wall.*)

That's ten and she has only just left her hovel.

(*thwack*)

Eleven times I've squashed the Hag, eleven times, what skill I have today.

(*silence as she watches*)

Like a roach she scuttles the road, I'll make it fifteen before she reaches the convent gates.

(*thwack*)

Damn!

(*thwack*)

Twelve!

(*thwack*)

Damn!

(*thwack*)

Thirteen! One can predict with such certainty this creature's habits, her path is as well furrowed as mine.

(*thwack*)

Again!

(*thwack, thwack*)

And Sister Agatha! My skill grows with the

OUR LADY OF SHADOWS

years. What gives she the hag today? What
distractions will be delivered? And what
                          devoured on the road?
I study every sinew of the world... outside, of
the world outside. And from the hawk eye
view, camera obscura, I watch and record the
neaptide of life.
Aloft low dizzy landscapes.
Hand stitched fields ebb and flow.
Trawled in my shroud
a galaxy of sheep, bone fenced,
fill my darkened chamber like heavenly bodies.
Lovers eclipsed in the mirrorlens, their
                  shadows my prisoners.
And... as a caged bird sings of escape I paint
                                      mine,
chart the years as they flourish and wither.
Mutatis mutandis.
And I feel my own body ripen.
As I paint the bloody birth of a lamb
the blush of a girl,
blueblack of a bird and the pain underfoot of a
horse pulling the dead weight of a
                          man's livelihood,
my breasts swell.
As the river swims to sea bluegreen
my blood waxes and wanes.
Will no one pluck me from the tree of
                          knowledge:
Must I grow mould?
Or does this cell preserve me like salt beef or
pickling onions?
Fully formed and straining to be born.
In my science I spy a silent shadow world
where godlike I learn my private crimes,
rhythms of fear and passions I can have
                                    none of.
I watch, I paint and I play squash the Hag!
(*thwack*)

OUR LADY OF SHADOWS

SCENE FIVE

"Round an island there below"

(*CATHERINE is having a shit. It falls down a long shaft. As she finishes a rattling and grunting sound comes from the grille in the cell door.*)

CATHERINE: Watching me, Hag? I know you're watching me.

HAG: (*grunts*)

CATHERINE: Watching me watch my shit, if you could you'd tell them, wouldn't you? Tell them I watch my shit, count the time till it reaches the bottom, watch it slide down the shaft clinging like leeches to the side. When the tide is low it stays and the stench fills my cell, mounds of my waste gather, expressing the time in waste.

HAG: (*grunts and offers her a parcel of food*)

CATHERINE: What's this?
Nectar from the Gods?
They sent you with pious offerings again?
Bread and wine.
The body and blood!
I could turn this bread into the body, no harder than sulphur into gold.
Instead I'll eat it.
Why carry you that tree? Will they crucify me?
Isn't it enough that I am caged for God?
Pass me the bread, Hag... pass it through, Hag.
I'm tired today and can't reach.
Come on, no one has removed your ears!

(*HAG starts to pass the bread through. CATHERINE leaps and grabs her arms, HAG is struggling and moaning.*)

CATHERINE: Let me out of here or I'll break your arms.... You might be built like a cart horse but I have the strength of despair. Fetch the key, I can see it.... For God's sake, pass it to me.... Come on, you can do it... fetch me that key, I see it.... Why should you have freedom with no tongue and a face like a plucked chicken? And me in here, my youth not half spent.... It's not fair!

(*The HAG breaks free and starts to fix a log across the bottom of the doorway. CATHERINE talks to her through the hole.*)

CATHERINE: If I said seal me up would you then release me? I clawed this hole overtime... longtime... and now you seal it with a felled tree. I beg for freedom and the fences get higher. (*clearly lying*) I clawed it for Christ, to make room for his coming, 'twas not for my escape Hag, I did not claw it to slip out slowly, to slip out slowly like a turd from my body.

HAG: (*grunts angrily at CATHERINE*)

CATHERINE: If you won't let me out, then take this to Sister Ignatious.... Take it.... Go on, take it.... Alright I'll put it down and you pick it up.... Oh! Don't look at me, Hag! Take it to Sister Ignatious, don't give it to any of the other nuns, and don't let anyone see you giving it to her....

(*She sees that the HAG is contemplating defiance.*)

If you don't, Hag! You know what they say about me in the village? It might be true. Go to it, Hag. With my science I can watch you. I can watch my gaoler as she infests the world. The watcher is watched. In my science I watch you pick up men like autumn leaves, I feel I should know what goes on in your hovel.

SCENE SIX

"Willows whiten, aspens quiver"

OUR LADY OF SHADOWS

(*CATHERINE is illuminating a manuscript from the image of the world reflected in her camera obscura. As she says this speech she can be heard drawing.*)

CATHERINE: Fresh emerald....

(*colouring grass quickly*)

Indian blue....

(*colouring sky with a different stroke*)

Vermilion....

(*long, straight brush strokes*)

My page imitates nature,
canal railed in....

(*as she traces line of canal*)

Field wicketed....

(*draws fences*)

Tall trees guard the river....

(*bold, strong strokes*)

Castle moated....

(*thick, dense colouring*)

Fenced in,
captive or safe?
My science reflects the world and I reflect it.
Living three shadows apart from the world.
Sealed in by bricks and mortar.

(*Spots HAG in camera obscura.*)

There she goes again!

(*thwack, she squashes her again*)

Scuttling like the creatures which share my prison. What is that she hides under her cloth? My craft can't mimic her... earth dug, her dark form is colourless.... Nature has painted her grey. I've no tools for this dark... *luminare, lumen, luminis.* Light, I paint the light in the world. These gems won't capture her dark. What is it that she hides, concealed like the treasure I hide in my tower? What carries she to her hovel? She paints her nails with my colours, eats bread meant for me and wears my burnishing tool from her ear as a trophy! Has she found Sister Ignatious? ...Oh why is my life dependent on a lice ridden Hag?

(*Thwack. She starts to draw again.*)

CATHERINE: Fish in fine silver.
White lead sheep firmly fenced.

(*drawing hard lines*)

Fettered flowers scarlet and saffron.
Blue green freighted sea.
And my image....

(*burnishing*)

Forged in the river's mirror
or a hawk's eye,
always a shadow.

(*mixing colours*)

Past blue hills, hag-coloured rocks hide dark passions unvoyaged.

(*scraping colours onto a palette*)

And clefts conceal ungirdled flowers.
Have I the colours for these sad shades?
Can I etch my escape on this unbridled landscape or must I paint my death and slip silently into my shroud to be borne from this place?...
Why gleam that mountain? Has a piece of heaven fallen into the wilderness?

SCENE SIX (a)

KNIGHT: (*He is riding his horse slowly, picking his way along a rocky track.*)

SCENE SEVEN

"She knows not what the curse may be"

(*CATHERINE is washing. She dips a cloth into water, wrings it out and then starts to wash the blood away from between her legs.*)

CATHERINE: Each bleed washed away marks time,
body moon pace,
washing away the stain.
As the moon dies I bleed, ready for time
to swell like a belly into another moon.
Round and round.
Round and round slowly the world moves,
round and round.
Slowly I walk round and round,
slowly, slowly, slowly.

(*realizes HAG is watching her*)

How long have you been there, Hag? How long? I should poke out your eyes, who said you could watch God in her heaven? My shadow's not half round yet so why have you come? Fattening me up like a pig in a pen?

(*The HAG hands her something.*)

This is not what I sent for! I asked you to bring me a windhawk to perch on my hand and circle my cage. What use is this?

(*The HAG laughs.*)

You laugh Hag, think this funny? Take pleasure in torment? She brings me a dead crow!

(to herself)

How can I mimic a bird in its death? Study its craft and master escape?

(*CATHERINE hurls the water through the grille at the HAG.*)

Wash the Hag! Wash her! I bet time doesn't stain heavy on her.

(*The HAG is annoyed and grunts and snarls at CATHERINE.*)

CATHERINE: Wet? The bear's been baited, here it comes claws at the ready, lice on guard.... Come on then, take on your tormentor! Come in here and fight me. Come in here.... Come on.... Oh go fuck a dog, Hag! If you won't release me the only use you are to me is to insult, and what pleasure is there in hurling words at someone who doesn't use them, and who can walk free, walk into the world? I know so much about the world. I know it's round, not flat.... There, you see, you didn't know that! It is! It is! And I've calculated how long it would take to circumnavigate. I have the knowledge of the world and yet have never been in it. Aristotle, Paracelsus, I thought I would retrace the steps of the great men. You are always the tormentor because the world is yours. In the world I illuminate even the colours are wrong, not flesh and blood. I'll paint the shadows of the world with blood.

(*She starts to scrape her blood onto pictures.*)

If paint won't do it maybe blood will. At least it's my fingers I have up my crotch Hag, my blood and my fingers!

OUR LADY OF SHADOWS

SCENE SEVEN (a)

KNIGHT: (*Now he is riding through a dark wood, his horse's hooves muffled by the deep leaves, the quietness accentuating the creak of leather and the sound of his armour as he moves.*)

SCENE EIGHT

"For often thro' the silent night"

(*The HAG is sleeping outside the cell door and snoring noisily. CATHERINE lights a candle which makes her shadow appear.*)

CATHERINE: The Hag sleeps noisily, *redemistri nos*, and you, drawn by my candle, sit solemnly before me, your dark shape mimics me. I wave, at myself, you torture me with your silence. If I don't move nor do you, if I scratch you do. So why can't you talk? Feed me words like sweetmeats. I know everything, the secrets of the universe, and yet I don't know you. Are you my darkened image shaped by the light? Or my soul ready for flight? I've turned sulphur to gold and yet I can't know you. You shadow the world which shadows me. I've balanced the light day and the night and yet I can't know you.
Hold me.
Or dance with me.
Dance!
Fill the cell with your jagged darkness.

(*She starts to dance round.*)

Spin over the walls of my tomb.
Dance, dance, dance!

(*getting faster*)

OUR LADY OF SHADOWS

Spin, swoop, swirl,
round and round.
Dance with me, shadow
a deadly dance.
A dance of death.
Help me dance myself to death.
Round and round,
round and round.

(*She starts to knock a few things over as she dances.*)

Hurl thybody with me till I die.
Spill me t'ward heaven.
I will die of dance and there is none to stop me.

(*She knocks over the candle that goes out then she falls on the floor exhausted.*)

Hell's teeth! The candle is over, my shadow is gone and I hawk sick.

(*despair*)

I can't even marshal my own death.

(*The HAG starts to make noise in her sleep.*)

CATHERINE: And now the Hag will start her wordless night
                                                                                         talk!
In her dreams she talks to the world.
In mine I range round it.
Unus Mundi.

SCENE EIGHT (a)

KNIGHT: (*The horse stops. The KNIGHT gets off with difficulty due to armour and has a piss. He gets back on and carries on riding.*)

SCENE NINE

(*CATHERINE is working on an illuminated*

manuscript which she is copying from what she can see of the world with her camera obscura.)

CATHERINE: (*mixing colours*) These colours are for heavenly toil! *Agnus Dei Qui peccata mundi.* Reapers and shepherds can't be painted in gold. Where is that abbot going? I should paint him shit brown. Does he know that God's putting his fat frame in her book?

(*She sees the HAG in the camera obscura.*)

CATHERINE: The hag crosses the causeway, dryshod. When Christ comes will he walk on the water or wait like the hag for the tide to be drawn?

(*The HAG is heard coming up the steps of the tower, out of breath.*)

CATHERINE: I paint my hatred hagways, bile skin, ash hair, piss-coloured eyes! With her beauty I illuminate Hag and Heaven! And nail her to the H. She even sounds like a beast of burden. What is it, Hag? Spying? Look! The blood has dried brown.

(*HAG holds a letter up and teases CATHERINE with it.*)

CATHERINE: Give that to me! You aren't that brave. Pass it through, stupid Hag, what use is it to you? (*as she takes letter*) Did she look well? Oh, why can't you speak?! Just nod, did she look well? (*pause*) Does that mean no? (*opens letter*) Words... words... words... marks on a page.

(*She starts to read it, the voice of SISTER IGNATIOUS reads the letter out loud.*)

SISTER IGN.: Catherine, I cannot do what you ask. We are all brides of Christ and must wait for his coming. I have waited fifty years, be patient.

CATHERINE: Be patient!

OUR LADY OF SHADOWS

SISTER IGN.: This communication is dangerous. The basilica is rebuilt and there is little sign of the fire but Holy Mother has not forgotten. Being an Anchoress is a less dangerous path to perfecttion.

CATHERINE: Alchemy is the only way.

SISTER IGN.: To prepare your soul through constant prayer and meditation.

CATHERINE: Is to rock oneself to death.

SISTER IGN.: In the tower you can concentrate your mind on God, discover his secrets.

CATHERINE: He has one secret.

SISTER IGN.: Many great women have followed your fate, sealed themselves up for God.

CATHERINE: I thought he loved me! As a child I remember you telling me stories, stories of great men, of my father, of Ulysses. I grew up hungry to discover the world like these men.

SISTER IGN.: I am on my way to heaven, God willing, too old to fight.

CATHERINE: And I am left here to rock my life to death. My father left me in a basket and now you leave me in this cradle of a grave. (*finishes the letter*) My hope rests on a gleam caught in my lens.

SCENE NINE (a)

KNIGHT: (*He is riding down a mountain.*)

SCENE TEN

"And there the surly village churls"

OUR LADY OF SHADOWS

(*CATHERINE is watching for the gleam in the hills with her camera obscura.*)

CATHERINE: Hag hills hide my hope.
Then a tiny gold glory gleams and hope flames again.
Will it have a tail?
Be it an angel?
Christ coming?
Or my father cast from the crusades in gold.
In limbo patrum I will its coming
Deeper, further, into my science come deeper, further.
Fear not, gleam, I'll not squash you like a flatfish!
Scuttle free today, Hag, my interest darts and dives the wildness with the grace of a windhawk.
Does it walk air?
Red cloaked market girls swirl like a river to the village and I haven't the heart to paint them.
I am bewitched by a firefly.
If I had a cloak that red I'd spin round and round till the goldbug be drawn to my flame.
And then I'd seal it in a jar.

SCENE TEN (a)

KNIGHT: (*He rides beside a brook. The horse drinks from it.*)

SCENE ELEVEN

"A funeral with plumes and lights"

(*CATHERINE is silently watching her image of the world.*)

SISTER IGN.: (*whispers*) Catherine! Catherine!

OUR LADY OF SHADOWS

CATHERINE: A sound?

SISTER IGN.: Catherine!

CATHERINE: My shadow?

SISTER IGN.: Come to the grille, quickly!

CATHERINE: Someone with words?

SISTER IGN.: Don't be afraid, Catherine, it is Sister Iggy.

CATHERINE: Put your hand through the bar, let me hold you.

SISTER IGN.: Is it the candlelight which makes you....

CATHERINE: What?

SISTER IGN.: Makes you look so....

CATHERINE: What?

SISTER IGN.: Your hair... like snakes... the dark has withered you.... Are you closer to God?

CATHERINE: If I answer right do you release me?

SISTER IGN.: I cannot release you.

CATHERINE: Then I'll answer truthfully and say I am God.... Why have you come if not to release me?

SISTER IGN.: Your crying creeps into my dreams.... What is that moving?

CATHERINE: God doesn't cry. The moon racing across the sky?

SISTER IGN.: On the floor... moving on the floor. Pictures? Ghosts?

CATHERINE: Shadows.

SISTER IGN.: Shadows are dark and indistinct... those colours?

CATHERINE: Shadows of the world.

SISTER IGN.: What witchcraft is this?

OUR LADY OF SHADOWS

CATHERINE: Science.

SISTER IGN.: Catherine, what have you been doing?

CATHERINE: Denied the world I have brought it to me.... See a funeral, bearers sweat under their load, weeping women carry torches to light the way.... I weave my own life. (*to herself*) And now I watch a gleam as it leaves the wilderness and travels the road, I will need a flagon to contain it.

SISTER IGN.: How did you do this... what devilment did you use?

CATHERINE: I built it... camera obscura... I have the world in my darkened chamber.

SISTER IGN.: Being alone has harmed you.

CATHERINE: My world is this room and so into this I bring all the experiences of life. And then I paint it with shit and blood.

SISTER IGN.: Is that what the stench is?

CATHERINE: Your colours are too bright for a shadow world. I paint the wildness and darkness, the shades between life and holiness... a darker world.

SCENE ELEVEN (a)

KNIGHT: (*He is trotting closer and closer now, the jangle of bit and bridle louder, the horse's breath harsher.*)

SCENE TWELVE

"A bow shot from her bowers-eaves"

(*CATHERINE is frantically looking for something in her cell.*)

CATHERINE: Damn the heavens, damn hell, it wasn't that

OUR LADY OF SHADOWS

long ago I used it. I remember painting the shepherd's hair with it.... Where has it gone?

(*She goes to the image of the world.*)

Stay vision, stay! Don't leave my science! I must capture this image on a page. Such brightness has come into my shadowland.

(*searching again*)

Have you painted your black teeth with it, Hag? May it turn to lead in your mouth! Where is it? Nothing but gold can paint this vision?

(*She turns back to the image.*)

Fields lie apart, it rides through, so erect... with power and beauty, balance and control. Radiantly enamelled, the sun coats it with glory. Even the river holds its image but as I do... a shadow. What is that smell? Does my body sweat hope? Hag, what's that you bring? Incense? Sister, sent you with those to drown my smell? She can mask my smell but not my hope!

SCENE TWELVE (a)

KNIGHT: (*He trots across a plank bridge over the faster flowing river. Sheep can be heard.*)

SCENE THIRTEEN

"The gemmy bridle glittered free"

(*CATHERINE is trying frantically to paint the KNIGHT.*)

CATHERINE: White page, virgin vellum.... (*with despair*) Dry parchment! Mark out his shape as he rides with such fury, too fast for his shadow! Illuminate the page with such light!

SCENE THIRTEEN (a)

KNIGHT: (*Now he rides through a barley field, making the barley swish, bridle jangle.*)

SCENE FOURTEEN

CATHERINE: (*still painting*) Why does this vision make me feel? It's line and symmetry, it's poise. Riding unchallenged.... How to paint passion?

SCENE FOURTEEN (a)

KNIGHT: (*He comes off the fields onto a hardened roadway and past a homestead.*)

SCENE FIFTEEN

"A mighty bugle hung"

CATHERINE: (*still painting*)

This image carved in gold.... Follow his line, its hard edge, how can anything so... make me feel....

SCENE FIFTEEN (a)

KNIGHT: (*Trotting on the roadway, he passes a slow wagon.*)

SCENE SIXTEEN

CATHERINE: Flesh and blood.... I feel flesh and blood. Mark

out his shape on my virgin page. He could break down these walls, find what's hidden inside. This quiet fury and passion.

SCENE SIXTEEN (a)

KNIGHT: (*Riding through a village, other road users quickly get out of his way.*)

SCENE SEVENTEEN

CATHERINE: (*She is pacing around image.*)

Havoc, he has caused havoc. The world jumps like a ball being shaken. Lightning cracks across the frame. Closer, come closer. This way....

(*HAG rattles grille.*)

CATHERINE: I don't want food today, Hag. Take it away! *Misere Nobus....*

(*back to image*)

CATHERINE: The world shakes as he rides,
My body shakes as he rides,
I follow you round and round,
Closer, come closer.

(*CATHERINE bangs on the bars.*)

CATHERINE: Toe rag... toerag, come here, Hag!

(*back to image*)

CATHERINE: See his face.... I can see his face... if I move my science closer, cut out the rest of the world. Come closer, find what treasures are hidden inside. Round and round.

(*HAG is at bars.*)

OUR LADY OF SHADOWS

CATHERINE: Let me out, Hag! Please! Get the key, pass it to me, I'll go on my knees, look you can have everything, my books....

(*hands HAG a jar*)

CATHERINE: This is the philosopher's stone, with this you can turn sulphur to gold. Please, Hag! Please! I'll tell you all that I know. I have seen my destiny ride before me. I must go and meet it.

(*She throws jar at bars.*)

CATHERINE: Spotted toad.... If I get out of here I'll cut off your ears and poke out your eyes.... I've got to see him in the world... not a shadow.

SCENE SEVENTEEN (a)

KNIGHT: (*He lifts the horse into a canter on the hard roadway, his armour jangles loudly. He passes the convent as the nuns are at vespers.*)

SCENE EIGHTEEN

"The mirror cracked from side to side"

(*CATHERINE is forcing open the shutters, banging and swearing as she attempts to open them.*)

CATHERINE: I will not be shuttered from the world!

(*She continues to force shutters.*)

CATHERINE: Come on! Come on! Damn and blast you! Come on, open, blast you open. I will see him. I will see him in the world. (*still forcing*) I've kept out the light for my science, but I've no time for shadows now. Shift, damn you, shift!

(*The shutter bar falls away. She opens the shutters and the world comes into her cell. Sounds of the river, the birds and the KNIGHT riding. From now on the KNIGHT riding can be heard all the time from inside her cell.*)

CATHERINE: The world smells so strong! The colours! It really was a shadow world... now rescued by the light! Flown through the shuttered window.... Where is he?! I'm looking at the world and he is not in it, was it a vision? Is he not real? Did my madness paint him? I can't walk around this world.... I can't walk round it.... I've let the shadow go and there's nothing. Over there! Over there! Gold flashes... it is him... I can see him... I can hear him! It is him! Gold against the blue, bold red across his breast... how my heart aches to be near him! Where is he going? Where does that path lead.... To the castle. He heads for the castle.... He has got to see me! He's got to! How can I make him see me? How is it you catch your men, Hag? What tricks do you use to trap them?

(*CATHERINE starts to sing the Paternoster.*)

CATHERINE: A knight with no ears! What to do? What to do? Do you seduce them with your yellow breasts, Hag?

(*She starts to tear off her clothes.*)

CATHERINE: I'll remove these bandages... release my body from its shroud.... He's got to see me, he's got to.

(*She continues to take off her clothes.*)

CATHERINE: If I... if I... peel off. Stand in the window. Got a body like this have you, Hag? Is that what draws men like leeches. Is it like this? Virgin skin unmarked. If I climb up in the window, he'll see me.

OUR LADY OF SHADOWS

(*CATHERINE starts to sing again.*)

CATHERINE: The air is touching my body, I can feel the winter sun stroke me and the wind between my legs.... I perch like a naked seacrow in the window calling... the dead have arisen! I want life.... Save this maiden from death.... Hag, he comes, he has seen me! Oh I wish I could pull my fingers through my hair... please God it doesn't look like the Hag's! He comes! I'll be out of here Hag, and then you'll be for it.

(*She shouts to the KNIGHT. He blows his bugle and gallops down the road towards her tower.*)

CATHERINE: Take me, out into the world.... Come to me.

(*KNIGHT rides across the causeway through the rising tidewater.*)

CATHERINE: This way... this way, that's right, he looks so hard in the layer of skin, is he made of gold? Will I be crushed?

(*KNIGHT reaches the island and leaps from his horse and climbs the steps of the tower. CATHERINE is beside herself.*)

CATHERINE: I can hardly breathe! He is coming... hurry, hurry.... I might die before you get here!

(*The KNIGHT starts to prise the log away from the door.*)

CATHERINE: He loosens the log.
Hagholds won't halt him!

(*The log falls away with a clatter. CATHERINE starts to shout through the hole.*)

CATHERINE: Fetch the key! Fetch the key! Above the door... there!

(*KNIGHT reaches key and unlocks door.*)

CATHERINE: I am being released... the tomb has opened!

I am unlocked!

(*Huge thump as the HAG hits the KNIGHT with the log. He falls down the steps of the tower crashing from stone step to step as he falls. Silence.*)

CATHERINE: No! No!

(*CATHERINE runs down steps to KNIGHT.*)

CATHERINE: No! The gleam is snuffed out, squashed by a Hag!

(*HAG attempts to slip away.*)

CATHERINE: I see you, Hag! I see you! It's too late, I'm out! Is that why you did this? Is that why? You lice-ridden arse! I guard your exit and now I'm going to tear you limb from limb! You've killed it, you've killed my saviour. Come on then, think you can get past me, do you?

(*CATHERINE dives at HAG. They fight fiercely with much grunting and snarling.*)

CATHERINE: Try and tear my flesh off! I'll tear everything off you! I'll swing you round and round by your hair....

(*swings her round*)

CATHERINE: Press your eyes out with my thumbs....

(*loud squeal of pain from HAG*)

CATHERINE: Hurt, does it? Poor Hag! My strength comes from hate Hag, you have no hope!

(*They continue to fight.*)

CATHERINE: Bare flesh is hard to grab, isn't it Hag? Your rags are easy to catch. Your turn to plead, is it? Did you listen to mine? You killed my hope and now I kill you.

(*The fight continues until they both collapse, exhausted and breathless.*)

OUR LADY OF SHADOWS

CATHERINE: Killing is not easy... yet, it died without a fight? And now his skin is coming off!

(*CATHERINE crawls over to KNIGHT and pulls the arm of his armour off.*)

He sheds his skin! The gold has gone! He is as soft as I inside, what pretence is this? Stay, Hag! You won't crawl far, I watch your every move. This creature sheds his skin!

(*She pulls his armour off.*)

CATHERINE: He is soft inside, not hard-edged.

(*still stripping him*)

CATHERINE: Like a snail without its shell!

(*strips him further*)

CATHERINE: Hag, I have eyes in the back of my head! That wall leads nowhere! My angel carved in gold is a snail without a home. His skin is lying in a heap beside him, the golden fleece. The snake has shed its skin and what abomination is this? Has Eve seen the serpent naked? I have been deceived! Hag, go and fetch my clothes. A story of escape has filled my mind.

(*as she kicks the armour to one side*)

CATHERINE: You are no more than me and I no less than you.

(*HAG returns with clothes.*)

CATHERINE: Here, help me! Help me! Don't look so dumb, Hag... that's right, pull it over his head, that's right... give me your shawl... there! Does the ferry boat still moor here? Good... help me carry him... come on. He is heavy, take his weight on your side... we'll drag him then.

(*They drag the KNIGHT, now dressed in her clothes, to the ferry boat.*)

OUR LADY OF SHADOWS

CATHERINE: Damn, I need his sword. Go fetch it, Hag, and hurry. The cold wind is nipping my arse and my breasts are frozen. Bring me his skin.

(*HAG runs off for sword.*)

CATHERINE: Winter flowers! Here let's lie them around you.

(*HAG returns with sword and armour half-heartedly contemplates defiance of CATHERINE with it.*)

CATHERINE: If you raise that sword to me I'll cut your breasts off and give them to our tarnished angel!

(*She hacks off her hair.*)

CATHERINE: Now I'm shorn.

(*She places her hair around the KNIGHT.*)

CATHERINE: How beautiful he looks, long hair becomes him... spread out the dress... (*shouts*) If you leave now Hag, I'll hunt you down! I'm not finished yet.

(*CATHERINE starts to put on his armour.*)

CATHERINE: I slide into the serpent's skin, like a sword into a sheath.... I will deceive the world as he did, act out his play. I can feel myself hardening like sulphur into gold, in this skin I go into the world! Let us send him on his new role.... Help me push.

(*They push the boat out into the water.*)

CATHERINE: And now for you, Hag. You are free to go, no need to tend to bitter prisoners. Stay in the tower. Make it your home. It has stone walls and a roof, you can learn all my secrets, paint your nails gold and keep men in bell jars. I am going out into the world to follow the footsteps of the great men.

OUR LADY OF SHADOWS

                (*CATHERINE mounts the KNIGHT'S horse with a bit of difficulty. The horse tosses its head at the unfamiliar rider.*)

CATHERINE: Circumnavigate the world.
                Discover new lands.
                Fight the Crusades.

END

                (Stage version: The only light until CATHERINE breaks open the shutters should come either from her candle when lit, weakly through the grille from the door when the HAG opens this and from the camera obscura image that is cast upon the floor [a coloured projection or occasionally moving gobo perhaps.])

Acknowledgements

The author would like to thank the following people: Duncan Gough for all his patience and inspiration; David Edgar for setting up the M.A. in Playwriting Studies at Birmingham University and for his kind support since; The Arts Council of Wales for their financial assistance over the years.

About the Author

Lucy Gough was born in London in 1958 and spent her early years in Beddgelert before the family settled in Bath where she attended a convent school. She left at fifteen without any qualifications and a year later returned to Wales, this time to Fishguard. There she followed an Open University course in Drama and in 1982 moved to Aberystwyth where she completed a degree in Drama in 1985. As part of her degree she wrote a play called *Bad Habits Die Hard*, about a naughty nun and started work on the play *Joanna* which was given a rehearsed reading by Made in Wales Theatre Company.

Other stage plays professionally performed include: *Catherine Wheel, By A Thread, As To Be Naked, Rushes, Stars* and *Wolfskin*. In 1994 *Crossing The Bar* was shortlisted for both the John Whiting Award and the BBC Wales Writer Of The Year Award. She has also had six commissions from BBC Radio: *Our Lady of Shadows* (Radio 3); *Head, The Red Room* (with material from Glyn Hughes), *Mermaids* (with material from Marina Warner) and *Canvas* (with material from Germaine Greer) for Radio 4, and *The Prophetess of Exeter* (a version of *Joanna*) for the World Service.

For the last four year she has been script-writing for Mersey TV's teen soap *Hollyoaks* and also currently lectures in Radio Drama at the Department of Theatre, Film and Television at the University of Wales, Aberystwyth. She is married and has three children.